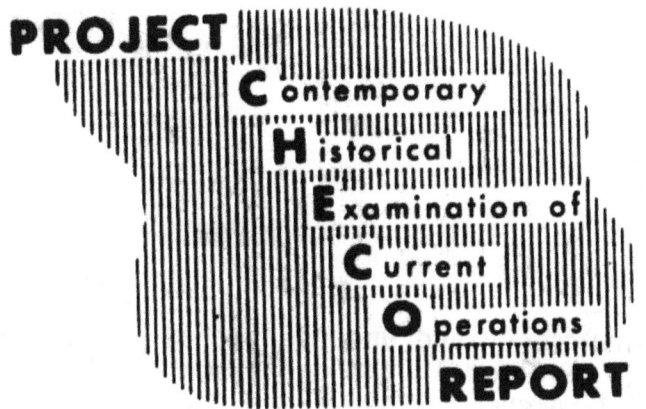

KONTUM: BATTLE FOR THE CENTRAL HIGHLANDS
30 MARCH - 10 JUNE 1972 (U)

27 OCTOBER 1972

HQ PACAF

Directorate of Operations Analysis
CHECO/CORONA HARVEST DIVISION

Prepared by:

CAPT PETER A.W. LIEBCHEN

Project CHECO 7th AF, DOAC

PROJECT CHECO REPORTS

The counterinsurgency and unconventional warfare environment of Southeast Asia has resulted in the employment of USAF airpower to meet a multitude of requirements. The varied applications of airpower have involved the full spectrum of USAF aerospace vehicles, support equipment, and manpower. As a result, there has been an accumulation of operational data and experiences that, as a priority, must be collected, documented, and analyzed as to current and future impact upon USAF policies, concepts, and doctrine.

Fortunately, the value of collecting and documenting our SEA experiences was recognized at an early date. In 1962, Hq USAF directed CINCPACAF to establish an activity that would be primarily responsive to Air Staff requirements and direction, and would provide timely and analytical studies of USAF combat operations in SEA.

Project CHECO, an acronym for Contemporary Historical Examination of Current Operations, was established to meet this Air Staff requirement. Managed by Hq PACAF, with elements at Hq 7AF and 7/13AF, Project CHECO provides a scholarly, "on-going" historical examination, documentation, and reporting on USAF policies, concepts, and doctrine in PACOM. This CHECO report is part of the overall documentation and examination which is being accomplished. It is an authentic source for an assessment of the effectiveness of USAF airpower in PACOM when used in proper context. The reader must view the study in relation to the events and circumstances at the time of its preparation--recognizing that it was prepared on a contemporary basis which restricted perspective and that the author's research was limited to records available within his local headquarters area.

ROBERT E. HILLER
Director of Operations Analysis
DCS/Operations

REPLY TO
ATTN OF: DOAD

27 October 1972

SUBJECT: Project CHECO Report, "Kontum: Battle for the Central Highlands, March 30-June 10, 1972" (U)

TO: SEE DISTRIBUTION PAGE

1. Attached is a SECRET NOFORN document. It shall be transported, stored, safeguarded, and accounted for in accordance with applicable security directives. SPECIAL HANDLING REQUIRED, NOT RELEASABLE TO FOREIGN NATIONALS. The information contained in this document will not be disclosed to foreign nations or their representatives. Retain or destroy in accordance with AFR 205-1. Do not return.

2. This letter does not contain classified information and may be declassified if attachment is removed from it.

FOR THE COMMANDER IN CHIEF

Alfred A. Picinich

ALFRED A. PICINICH, Lt Colonel, USAF
Chief, CHECO/CORONA HARVEST Division
Directorate of Operations Analysis
DCS/Operations

1 Atch
Proj CHECO Rprt, (S/NF),
27 Oct 72

DISTRIBUTION LIST

1. SECRETARY OF THE AIR FORCE

   a. SAFAA 1
   b. SAFLL 1
   c. SAFOI 2
   d. SAFUS 1

2. HEADQUARTERS USAF

   a. AFNB 1

   b. AFCCS
      (1) AFCCN 1
      (2) AFCVC 1
      (3) AFCHOS 2

   c. AFCSA
      (1) AF/SAG 1
      (2) AF/SAMI 1

   d. AFIGO
      (1) AFOSI/IVOA . . . 3
      (2) IGS 1

   e. AFINATC 5

   f. AFACMI 1

   g. AFODC
      (1) AFPRC 1
      (2) AFPRE 1
      (3) AFPRM 1

   h. AFPDC
      (1) AFDPW 1

   i. AFRD
      (1) AFRDP 1
      (2) AFRDQ 1
      (3) AFRDQPC 1
      (4) AFRDR 1
      (5) AFRDQL 1

   j. AFSDC
      (1) AFLGX 1
      (2) AFLGM 1
      (3) AFLGF 1
      (4) AFLGS 1
      (5) AFSTP 1

   k. AFDAD 1

   l. AFXO 1
      (1) AFXOD 1
      (2) AFXODC 1
      (3) AFXODD 1
      (4) AFXODL 1
      (5) AFXOOG 1
      (6) AFXOSL 1
      (7) AFXOV 1
      (8) AFXOOSN 1
      (9) AFXOOSO 1
      (10) AFXOOSS 1
      (11) AFXOOSV 1
      (12) AFXOOTR 1
      (13) AFXOOTW 1
      (14) AFXOOSZ 1
      (15) AF/XOXAA 6
      (16) AFXOXXG 1

3. MAJOR COMMAND

   a. TAC

      (1) HEADQUARTERS
          (a) OA 1
          (b) DOC 1
          (c) DREA 1
          (d) IN 1

      (2) AIR FORCES
          (a) 12AF
              1. DOO 1
              2. IN 1
          (b) 19AF(IN) 1
          (c) USAFSOF(DO) . . . 1

      (3) WINGS
          (a) 1SOW(DOI) 1
          (b) 23TFW(DOI) 1
          (c) 27TRW(DOI) 1
          (d) 33TFW(DOI) 1
          (e) 35TFW(DOI) 1
          (f) 314TAW(DOI) . . . 1
          (g) 347TRW(DOI) . . . 1
          (h) 67TRW(DOI) 1
          (i) 316TAW(DOX) . . . 1
          (k) 317TFW(DOI) . . . 1
          (l) 474TFW(DOI) . . . 1
          (m) 516TAW(DOX) . . . 1
          (n) 4403TFW(DOI) . . . 1
          (o) 58TAC FTR TNG WG . 1
          (p) 354TFW(DOI) . . . 1

      (4) TAC CENTERS, SCHOOLS
          (a) USAFTAWC(IN) . . . 1
          (b) USAFTFWC(DR) . . . 1
          (c) USAFAGOS(EDA) . . 1

   b. SAC
      (1) HEADQUARTERS
          (a) DOX 1
          (b) XPX 1
          (c) LG 1
          (d) IN 1
          (e) NR 1
          (f) HO 1

      (2) AIR FORCES
          (a) 2AF(INA) 1
          (b) 8AF(DOA) 2
          (c) 15AF(INCE) . . . 1

   c. MAC
      (1) HEADQUARTERS
          (a) DOI 1
          (b) DOO 1
          (c) CSEH 1
          (d) MACOA 1
          (e) 60MAWG(DOXPI) . 1

      (2) MAC SERVICES
          (a) AWS(HO) 1
          (b) ARRS(XP) 1

   d. ADC
      (1) HEADQUARTERS
          (a) DO 1
          (b) DOT 1
          (c) XPC 1

      (2) AIR DIVISIONS
          (a) 25AD(DOI) . . . 1
          (b) 20AD(DOI) . . . 1

   e. ATC
      (1) DOSPI 1
      (2) DPX 1

f. AFSC
   (1) HEADQUARTERS
       (a) XRP 1
       (b) SDA 1
       (c) HO 1
       (d) ASD(RWST) 1
       (e) ESD(XRL) 1
       (f) RADC(DOT) 1
       (g) ADTC(CCN) 1
       (h) ADTC(DLOSL) . . . 1
       (i) ESD(YWA) 1
       (j) AFATL(DL) 1

g. USAFSS
   (1) HEADQUARTERS
       (a) AFSCC(SUR) . . . 2

h. USAFSO
   (1) HEADQUARTERS
       (a) CSH 1

i. PACAF
   (1) HEADQUARTERS
       (a) DP 1
       (b) IN 1
       (c) XP 2
       (d) CSH 1
       (e) DC 1
       (f) LG 1
       (g) DOAD 6

   (2) AIR FORCES
       (a) 5AF
           1. CSH 1
           2. XP 1
           3. DO 1
       (b) 7AF
           1. DO 1
           2. IN 1
           3. DOCP 1
           4. DOAC 2
       (c) 13AF(CSH) 1
       (d) 7/13AF(CHECO) . . 1

   (3) AIR DIVISIONS
       (a) 313AD(DOI) 1
       (b) 314AD(XP) 1
       (c) 327AD(IN) 1

      (4) WINGS
         (a) 8TFW(DOEA) 1
         (b) 56SOW(WHD) 1
         (c) 366TFW(DO) 1
         (d) 388TFW(DO) 1
         (e) 405TFW(DOI) 1
         (f) 432TRW(DOI) 1
         (g) 1st Test Sq(DA) . . 1

      (5) OTHER UNITS
         (a) Task Force ALPHA(IN) 1

j. USAFE
   (1) HEADQUARTERS
      (a) DOA 1
      (b) DOLO 1
      (c) DOO 1
      (d) XP 1

   (2) AIR FORCES
      (a) 3AF(DO) 1
      (b) 16AF(DO) 1

   (3) WINGS
      (a) 50TFW(DOA) 1
      (b) 20TFW(DOI) 1
      (c) 401TFW(DCOI) 1
      (d) 513TAW(DOI) 1

4. SEPARATE OPERATING AGENCIES
   a. ACIC(DOP) 2

   b. AFRES(XP) 2

   c. 3825AU
      1. ACSC-DAA 1
      2. AUL(SE)-69-108 . . . 2

      3. HOA 2

   d. ANALYTIC SERVICES, INC . 1

   e. AFAG(THAILAND) 1

5. MILITARY DEPARTMENTS, UNIFIED AND SPECIFIED COMMANDS, AND JOINT STAFFS

    a. COMUSJAPAN/J3 1
    b. CINCPAC (J301) 2
    c. CINCPACFLT (Code 321) 1
    d. COMUSKOREA (ATTN: J-3) 1
    e. COMUSMACTHAI/MACTJ3 1
    f. COMUSMACV (TSCO) 1
    g. COMUSTDC (J3) 1
    h. USCINCEUR (ECJB) 1
    i. CINCLANT (CL) 1
    j. CHIEF, NAVAL OPERATIONS 1
    k. COMMANDANT, MARINE CORPS (ABQ) 1
    l. CINCONAD (NHSV-M) 1
    m. DEPARTMENT OF THE ARMY (ASM-D) 1
    n. JOINT CHIEFS OF STAFF (J3RR&A) 1
    o. JSTPS 1
    p. SECRETARY OF DEFENSE (OASD/SA) 1
    q. CINCSTRIKE (STS) 1
    r. CINCAL (RCJ3-A) 1
    s. MAAG-CHINA (MGOT-LA) 1
    t. U.S. DOCUMENTS OFFICE, HQ ALLIED FORCES NORTHERN EUROPE . . . 1
    u. USMACV (MACJ031) 1

6. SCHOOLS

    a. Senior USAF Representative, National War College 1
    b. Senior USAF Representative, Armed Forces Staff College 1
    c. Senior USAF Representative, Naval Amphibious School 1
    d. Senior USAF Representative, Naval Amphibious School 1
    e. Senior USAF Rep, U.S. Marine Corps Education Center 1
    f. Senior USAF Representative, U.S. Naval War College 1
    g. Senior USAF Representative, U.S. Army War College 1
    h. Senior USAF Rep, U.S. Army C&G Staff College 1
    i. Senior USAF Representative, U.S. Army Infantry School 1
    j. Senior USAF Rep, USA JFK Cen for Mil Asst 1
    k. Senior USAF Representative, U.S. Army Field Artillery School . 1
    l. Senior USAF Representative, U.S. Liaison Office 1
    m. Senior USAF Rep, U.S. Army Armor School, Comd and Staff Dept . 1

7. SPECIAL

    a. The RAND Corporation 1

TABLE OF CONTENTS

	Page
LIST OF ILLUSTRATIONS	xii
ABOUT THE AUTHOR	xiii
FOREWORD	xiv

CHAPTER I. BACKGROUND TO INVASION 1

    Intelligence Estimates: The Central Highlands as the
        Primary Target 1
    The Surprises: Tanks and Conventional Tactics 3

CHAPTER II. THE OFFENSIVE BEGINS: EARLY NVA SUCCESSES 8

    The Enemy Probes the Highlands 8
    Air Keeps the Enemy Off-Balance 11
    The Attacks Increase and Diversify 12
    Loss of FSB Charlie 14
    Enemy Objectives 15
    The Enemy Offensive Continues 16
    Tanks at Tan Canh/Dak To 17
    Why Did Tan Canh/Dak To Fall? 23
    Developments Through 30 April 1972 25

CHAPTER III. MAY 1972: THE ASSAULTS ON KONTUM CITY 33

    Function of the II DASC 33
    The Offensive Continues 34
    The "Rockpile" Operation 36
    Closing in on Kontum City 37
    Maneuvering for the Attack 40
    The First Attack on Kontum City 42
    Air Frustrates a Major Enemy Assault 47
    Preludes to the Final Effort 49
    All-Out Attack on Kontum City 51
    The Enemy Withdraws 62
    The Death of John Paul Vann 69

		Page

CHAPTER IV. USAF AND VNAF AIR IN THE DEFENSE OF THE CENTRAL
HIGHLANDS 71

    The Role of the B-52s 71
    The Role of U.S. TACAIR 73
    The Role of the U.S. Gunships 75
    Other Air Resources 78
    Problems With BDA/KBA 79
    The SA-7 Threat 80
    VNAF Performance 82
    Air Power and the Battle for Kontum 84

CHAPTER V. CONCLUSION 85

    A New ARVN Aggressiveness 85
    Enemy Reactions and Future Plans 88

APPENDIX

    I.   MR II Flown Sorties - Mar/Apr 1972 90

   II.   MR II Flown Sorties - Apr/May 1972 91

  III.   MR II Flown Sorties - May 1972 92

   IV.   MR II Flown Sorties - June 1972 93

    V.   MR II KBA April 1972 94

   VI.   MR II Tanks Des/Dam April 1972 95

  VII.   MR II Trucks Des/Dam April 1972 96

 VIII.   MR II KBA May 1972 97

   IX.   MR II Tanks Des/Dam May 1972 98

    X.   MR II Trucks Des/Dam May 1972 99

   XI.   MR II KBA June 1972 100

  XII.   MR II Tanks Des/Dam June 1972 101

 XIII.   MR II Trucks Des/Dam June 1972 102

	Page
XIV. MR II Order of Battle (N) 30 April 1972	103
XV. MR II Order of Battle (N) 31 May 1972	104
FOOTNOTES	105
GLOSSARY	116

LIST OF ILLUSTRATIONS

Figure		Page
1.	South Vietnam Military Regions	7
2.	Battle for Tan Canh/Dak To	18
3.	MR II Major Roads and Airfields	19
4.	Air Force Fighter Bombers Destroy Tank at Dak To	28
5.	Spectre Destroys Trucks on Route 14	29
6.	Kontum City	41
7.	Refugees Flee Kontum City	54
8.	ARVN 23RD Division Gunners Defend the Perimeter	59
9.	ARVN Soldiers Root Out the Enemy in Kontum City	60

ABOUT THE AUTHOR

Captain Liebchen received his commission in the USAF upon graduation from Officer Training School at Lackland AFB, Texas, in December 1967. He had completed a Master's Degree in Modern European History at Rutgers University prior to entering the Air Force. Since that time he has served as an Administrative Officer, a Squadron Commander and as Chief of the Language Training Branch at Chanute AFB, Illinois. Immediately before becoming a CHECO writer, Captain Liebchen was an Instructor in German at the United States Air Force Academy. He plans to return there upon the completion of his SEAsia assignment.

FOREWORD

Kontum: Battle for the Central Highlands is one of a series of Project CHECO reports on the North Vietnamese Army (NVA) 1972 Offensive. Predicted by most observers as the "logical" focal point of any new enemy offensive, action in the Central Highlands of Military Region II (MR II) remained disquietingly inconclusive until mid-May. While major battles at Quang Tri in MR I and at An Loc in MR III captured most of the headlines, a series of engagements at Tan Canh/Dak To and the smaller Fire Support Bases (FSBs) along "Rocket Ridge" set the scene for the major attacks on Kontum City of 14 and 24 May 1972.

This report focuses primarily on the action in Kontum and Pleiku provinces, although significant events in other areas of MR II are mentioned. The almost immediate loss of Tam Quan, Hoai Nhon and Hoaian districts in the east coast province of Binh Dinh rendered the defense of the Central Highlands extremely critical since the loss of Kontum and Pleiku would, in effect, have split South Vietnam in two.

The role of United States and South Vietnamese airpower in preventing defeat in the Central Highlands is the dominant theme of this report. In many cases, on-the-scene interviews with participants in the battles form the basis for personal assessments of the key role airpower played in the defense of Kontum City; however, tables and charts of sorties flown and Bomb Damage Assessment (BDA) are provided in an appendix.

I would like to acknowledge my appreciation to all II DASC personnel for their aid in the preparation of this report. Special appreciation is reserved for Colonel Donald B. Swenholt, Major General Alton D. Slay's* personal representative at II DASC (Direct Air Support Center) during the battles for Kontum City. The bulk of Chapter III is based on Colonel Swenholt's on-the-scene reports.

*Former Director of Operations, Headquarters 7th Air Force.

CHAPTER I

BACKGROUND TO INVASION

Intelligence Estimates: The Central Highlands As The Primary Target*

Late in 1971, Allied intelligence officials became increasingly aware of and concerned about stepped-up NVA activity in the tri-border area near South Vietnam's Central Highlands. All-source intelligence indications in Base Area 609 (that area on which Cambodia, Laos and the Republic of Vietnam [RVN] all border) caused some analysts to speculate that the area was in danger of sinking from its saturation with enemy supplies and equipment.1/

The USAF air interdiction campaign, labeled COMMANDO HUNT VII, began early in November 1971. It attempted to minimize the flow of supplies from North Vietnam (NVN) through the Laotian panhandle into South Vietnam, but decreased strike sorties (due to the U.S. drawdown) coupled with the increasing diversity of the enemy road network weakened the effort. The Viet Cong (VC)-designated B-3 front (consisting primarily of Kontum and Pleiku provinces), received many of the benefits of the enemy's stockpiling efforts.

Early in 1972 U.S. officials publicly revealed that the 320th NVA Division, in concert with the 2d NVA Division, had infiltrated to the B-3

---

*Unless otherwise noted, material for this chapter comes from the CHECO report U.S. Air Deployments In Response to the NVA 1972 Offensive. Chapter II entitled "Intelligence Estimates and Military Situation," based on classified and unclassified sources, was particularly helpful.

1

Front from Laos. This focused attention on the Central Highlands, where the Army of the Republic of Vietnam (ARVN) forces were weakest, the population sparse, and government control tenuous. Neither the 22d nor the 23d ARVN Divisions was highly regarded," and both "showed a marked reluctance to mount long-range patrols outside their artillery fans."[2/]

On 15 January 1972 heavy B-52 raids, averaging over nine sorties per day, began concentrating in the B-3 Front area, where some 30-50,000 NVA troops were believed to be concentrating. The dynamic John Paul Vann, Senior U.S. Advisor in MR II, expected any new enemy offensive to hit hardest in Kontum province with Dak To and Ben Het as major targets. He was not too worried about demonstrated ARVN weaknesses such as the inadequate command and control lines; nor did he seem too concerned about serious NVA attempts to take Pleiku or Kontum. Vann felt that any attack would be halted by massive air and artillery power rather than ARVN because, "I'm enough of a realist that I'm not going to ask the ARVN to do what they won't do." He further predicted that the enemy was prepared to lose one fifth of the approximately 50,000 troops reportedly ready to attack in MR I and MR II.

Most estimates predicted the start of the offensive during Tet, the lunar New Year holiday, which fell on 14 February. Although increased enemy activity was noted in many regions, no unanimity existed in the interpretation of these moves. Some felt the offensive had already begun. Others saw the probes as a prelude to a major offensive due between July and September and timed to coincide with the U.S. presidential campaign.

Still others predicted March or April based on captured NVA documents and prisoner of war (POW) interrogations. Vann, who still maintained that the initial blow would be struck in MR II, had settled initially on 21 February as the start of the offensive; but later changed this to late March. On 27 March he predicted the offensive would begin within seven days. Events were to prove him correct.[3/]

The Surprises: Tanks and Conventional Tactics

The NVA use of tanks in MR II was anticipated, but the volume and diversity of types encountered was not. In addition to the Soviet-built T-54 and its variants, the offensive marked the appearance of the PT-76 (a light amphibious tank) and the ZSU-57/2 (equipped with twin 57mm antiaircraft artillery (AAA) and target-acquisition radar). A later estimate stated that approximately 400 enemy tanks were in-place in MR II at the beginning of the offensive. While intelligence experts were aware that tanks were present, obtaining confirmed photo reconnaissance of them in any quantity proved an elusive goal. Nevertheless agent and occasionally Forward Air Controller (FAC) reports noted unusual activity and included occasional references to tanks. A USAF FAC who flew in the tri-border region during early 1972 stated that[4/]

> *we noticed a lot of activity on the trails. They were building new roads; a lot of truck traffic in Laos and Cambodia. They were constructing storage areas, but we could never get any air to put on them. . . . For 6 months before the current offensive we worked almost exclusively with VNAF. We'd get one or two U.S. frags per day into MR II; then the offensive started and we got swarms of it that we couldn't use.*

Another Covey FAC flying the same region during the above period contended that[5/]

> *at the time most of the air assets were going further up north - on the trail. We just did not have the air assets available to us. . . . We'd report our sightings to our intel shop. Some of the targets were struck, but quite a bit of it did get through for lack of air resources.*

The latter FAC added that he personally sighted six tanks, but they were outside his area of operations (AO), and the Rules of Engagement (ROE) prevented his calling strikes on them. He noted that[6/]

> *we had O-2's stationed at Pleiku and their specific task was flying the tri-border area. There was quite a bit of evidence of troop buildups, moving in equipment and supplies by truck, and tank escorts for the trucks. . . . We saw evidence of it coming down the trail, and where the Laos/Cambodian border is, there's a fork in the trail - one going to Cambodia and one going to South Vietnam. We noticed several new roads that used to be paths, with heavy tank and truck traffic.*

While reduced U.S. air assets might be a partial explanation for the limited detection and destruction of enemy tanks, geography proved to be the greatest liability in detecting tank concentration. Much of the sophisticated and extensive road network carved out by the enemy had been constructed in areas impenetrable from the air. One USAF officer at II Direct Air Support Center (DASC) in Pleiku noted a[7/]

> *large area northeast of us here. . . . it's all triple canopy. That's the theory of how the enemy infiltrated, rather than coming down through Ben*

4

> *Het and that area in the western approaches. He went from Cambodia/Laos well north of Kontum into that triple canopy stuff, and worked his way down to the northeast. We fly over it days, but we can't see anything. The only way is to put people in it on the ground to see what's going on.*

In addition to aerial reconnaissance, intelligence data and ARVN patrols confirmed the enemy buildup in MR II. An ARVN airborne brigade added to the 22d and 23d Divisions led to more aggressive patrols from FSB's Five and Six resulting in almost daily contacts with the enemy. Signs, such as VC/NVA logistics and troop movements, pointed to MR II and the Central Highlands as the major enemy objective.[8] The crack NVA 320th Division, with its subordinate 48th, 52nd and 64th regiments, joined the 2d Division and the indigenous VC units to pose a threat to the area. On the east coast of MR II, particularly in Binh Dinh province, the NVA 3d Division bolstered the local VC units.[9] The size and composition of enemy divisions varied with the part of the country and the specific area in which they operated. The NVA 320th Division had an estimated 6,875 soldiers before the heavy contact at Kontum; other divisions ran higher, while some had as few as 4,500.[10]

The estimated enemy strength in the Central Highlands was put at some 20,000 men organized into:[11]

1 Corps (B-3 Front)
2 Infantry Division Headquarters
   (HQs) - NVA 320th and 2nd Divisions
8 Infantry Regiment (Reg) HQ's
29 Infantry Battalion (Bn) HQ's
2 Tank Bn's (PT-76, T-54)
1 Artillery Reg. HQ's

13 Artillery Bn's (105/85mm)
1 Bn 130mm
1 Bn 122/107 rockets
3 Bn 82, 120, 160mm mortars
3 Bn 12.7, 14.5, 37mm AAA
4 Bn 57/75mm recoilless rifles.

The scale and composition of the enemy build-up clearly indicated that any new offensive would be primarily an NVA operation, conducted along the lines of classical and conventional warfare. The unprecedented NVA invasion of late March gave final proof to the RVN claim that the rebellion in the south was not indigenous, as claimed by the Viet Cong and their allies; but deliberately fomented, controlled and executed by North Vietnam.[12/]

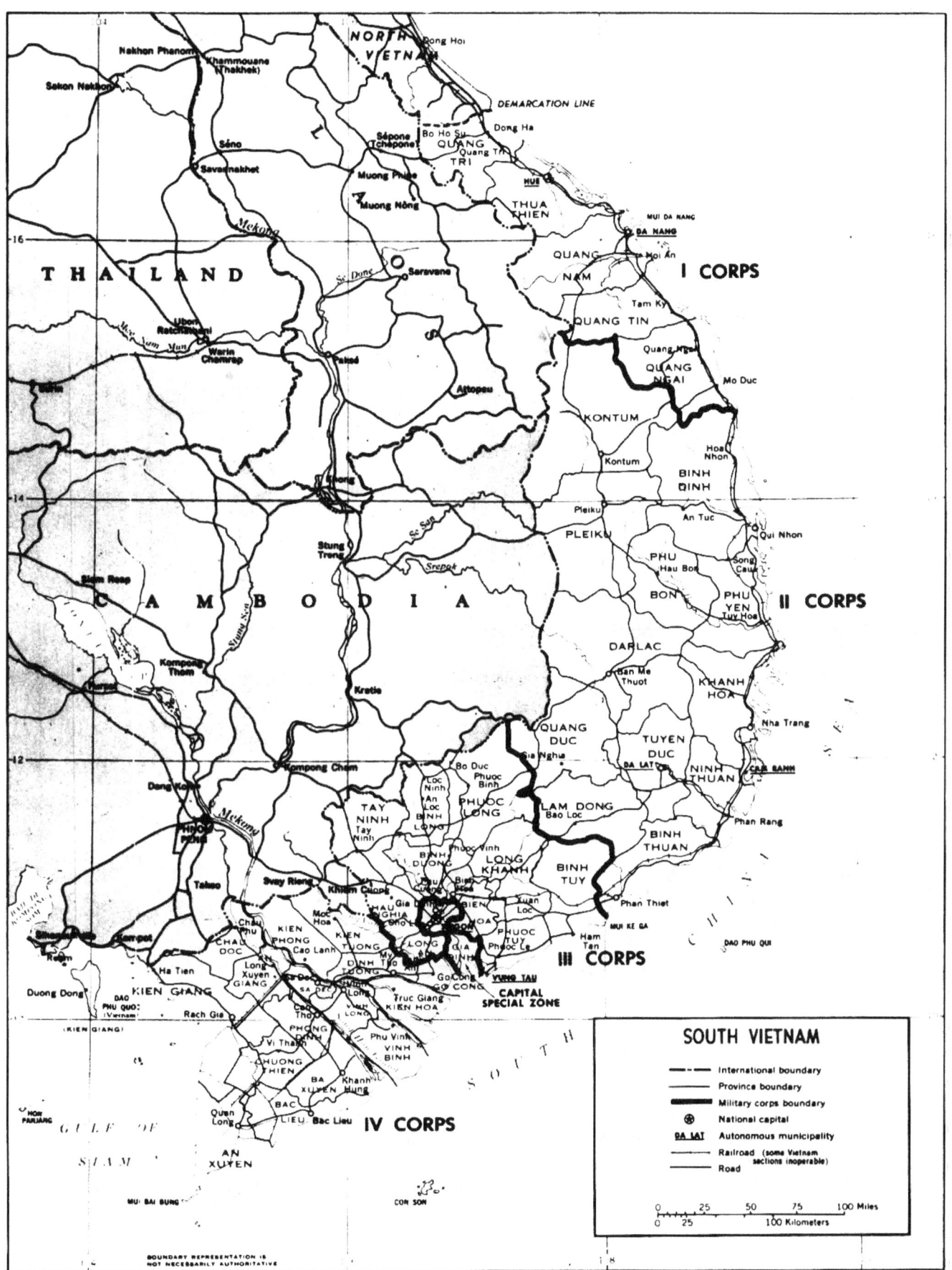

FIGURE 1

CHAPTER II

THE OFFENSIVE BEGINS: EARLY NVA SUCCESSES

The Enemy Probes the Highlands

Occasional ARVN contacts with the enemy increased in number and intensity as March began. VNAF and USAF aircraft, operating in what was once considered a permissive environment, noted a definite increase in AAA activity, especially in north-western Kontum province. A U.S. Army advisor to the VNAF helicopter force states that for his unit the offensive "started on March 22nd when he had 11 ships damaged in one day."[13/] In general terms, however, no all-out attack had as yet been unleashed. There were several reasons why the general offensive did not strike the Central Highlands first. Although the enemy had established lines of communication (LOC) in the area, seasoned MR II analysts felt that "the NVA have had a great deal of difficulty coordinating, and it didn't appear as if they had everything set up, ready to go."[14/] Added to possible internal problems, B-52 strikes and the ARVN harassed the enemy. A visual reconnaissance (VR) of a B-52 strike area on 23 March indicated that a probable enemy command post (CP) area had been hit, and that a forward element of the B-3 front had probably been the victim of the giant bombers.[15/]

On 28 March fighting broke out when[16/]

> *the enemy locked in combat with 23rd Ranger Bn . . . 20 kms north of Kontum City. The rangers fought well, linked up with another ranger unit on the 29th after fighting every step of the way, often hand to hand.*

> *The extraction of wounded rangers was marked by professionalism and extreme bravery on the part of senior VNAF officers, in particular wing and squadron commanders, who flew repeatedly into heavy enemy fire. The CO of the 235th Squadron continued flying support despite painfully severe face wounds caused by shattered plexiglass incurred from heavy ground fire. Documents and prisoners confirmed that the two day donnybrook with the rangers had cost the B-3 Front's 28th Regiment 338 KIA, a casualty figure which was only a harbinger of things to come. Any suspicion that these were not NVA regulars was dispelled by their appearance, which saw young Vietnamese dressed smartly in green and Khaki uniforms. Ranger losses were set at 33 KIA and 57 WIA.*

Heavy attacks by fire (ABFs) on the Fire Support Bases lining the "Rocket Ridge" area west of Kontum City and southwest of Tan Canh began on 30 March at the same time enemy activity began in MR I at Quang Tri and MR III at Lac Long. [17/] By 1 April, sporadic contacts with the enemy had occurred as far south as 19 km WSW of Kontum City, where ARVN Ranger elements engaged an estimated platoon at 1125H. The clashes along Rocket Ridge continued, and by 2 April some 12 ABF's had occurred at eight of the 10 FSBs stretching from Dak To to Kontum City. [18/] Contacts near FSB Charlie (ZB013097) lasted for five hours, and involved elements of the NVA 320th Division. On 3 April, a FSB 20 KM south of Dak To reported enemy losses as 353 Killed in Action (KIA) with 200 of that number Killed by Air (KBA), primarily VNAF tactical air (TACAIR) and U.S. helicopter gunships. [19/] Pleiku Air Base received an ABF that same day, as did FSB 421.

The 3 April attack on Phung Hoang airfield,* executed by sappers from the D-10 Sapper Bn of the 2d NVA Division, added a new element to the battle

*Near Dak To.

and left no doubt that the NVA considered the highlands a major objective.[20/] Prisoners captured during this assault stated that the attacks on the B-3 front were designed to seize Kontum Province as a base for the NVA 2d Division. The NVA 320th Division was to attack Kontum City. Further POW statements alleged that the VC/NVA campaign in the highlands was directed by Hanoi's General Giap, who promised 300 tanks for the B-3 front.[21/]

Probing attacks continued for the next several days, primarily in the Rocket Ridge area. Dak To I was fired on, and Dak To airfield was hit by sappers, who destroyed a fuel bladder. Aircraft reported heavy AAA fire north of Dak To, and two ARVN tanks were destroyed by recoilless rifle fire one kilometer west of the town.[22/] On 5 April, FSB Zulu was hit by a light ground probe, and some 15 incidents were reported in Kontum Province. Pleiku Province reported some three ABFs on that day, one of which consisted of a rocket attack on MR II HQ in Pleiku City. Of the five 122mm rockets launched against this target, four were duds and the fifth caused no damage. The ARVN military command now expected large-scale enemy attacks to come soon, particularly in the areas north of Kontum City and Dak To. Other probable targets were along Highway QL14 between Kontum and Pleiku cities, and on the lifeline road between Kontum City and Tan Canh/Dak To. In the eastern province of Binh Dinh, the enemy made rapid strides to consolidate his holdings in the three northern districts, and threatened to cut Highway 19, a vital link between Qui Nhon and Pleiku cities.[23/] On 6 April, with a relative lull in enemy activity throughout Kontum Province, ARVN units launched a counter-offensive on enemy positions in the Dak To area. Such actions may have been just what the enemy desired, since documents captured shortly thereafter indicated that the NVA 320th Division was regrouping and waiting for ARVN troops to make large-scale commitments away from the relative safety of their base camps.[24]

On 6 April the enemy, by attacking Pleiku airfield with 5x122mm rocket fire, renewed their offensive effort. At 0200H on 7 April FSB Mike, located 4 km from Vo Dinh in Kontum Province, reported a sapper attack. FSB Metro (ZB115045) repulsed an attack with the aid of VNAF AC-47 gunships, and Popular Force (PF) elements were harassed on Highways 14 and 19. The latter action resulted in explosives damage to bridge #29 on Route 19 (BR185520). On Route 14, ARVN Forces captured four 12.7mm AAA weapons and two 75mm recoilless rifles.[25]

Air Keeps the Enemy Off-Balance

The record of the first week of the offensive showed that the airpower upset the enemy's equilibrium and blunted the probing efforts. For example, heavy enemy fire from the surrounding high ground kept Dak To airfield closed until 11 April, when a B-52 strike forced elements of the NVA 2d Division to retrench. The airfield quickly reopened.[26] Friendly patrols found many groups of enemy KBA. For example, it was reported on 8 April that:[27]

> *In Kontum Province yesterday, ARVN elements on an ARC LIGHT BDA mission found 92 enemy KBA and 100 bunkers destroyed within 4 km of ZA225980 N W of Kontum City.*

and:

> *ARVN elements on a sweep operation 24 km N W of
> Kontum City (at ZB049038) discovered 80 enemy bodies
> killed by previous artillery and TACAIR strikes.*

A Regional Force (RF) patrol reported 92 KBA at ZA220020 near Kontum City, and a Controlled American Source (CAS) Field Comment summarized the effect air had on the invaders by adding: "Indications continue that massive U.S. air attacks are keeping the enemy off-balance on the B-3 Front."[28/]

The B-52 ARC LIGHT strikes proved especially potent in devastating enemy troop and supply concentrations. Many POWs stated that "the bombings . . . were sources of great demoralization among the (enemy) troops."[29/]

The Attacks Increase and Diversify

At 0050H on 9 April, sappers, possibly from the 407th VC Local Force, attacked the main U.S. housing and ammunition storage area at Cam Ranh Bay. Portions of the ammunition dumps were lost, but far worse was the loss of four Americans KIA and 20 U.S. personnel wounded, six seriously. The enemy had widened his AO to include the south eastern coastal region of MR II.[30/]

In the highlands, ARVN elements clashed several times with units of the 2d NVA Division in the area north of Route 512, within 6 km of Dak To II. Sweeping 14 km north of Tan Canh, they found some 62 enemy KBA. Four destroyed enemy bunkers with 45 bodies were found 25 km northwest of

Kontum City, while a complex of 100 destroyed bunkers with 92 KBA was discovered 10 km north of the city.[31/]

The next few days saw clashes at the FSBs and outposts both north and south of Kontum City. Kontum City received 12X122mm on 9 April with little damage reported, and Dak To airfield was hit by a series of 82mm mortars. ARVN units continued to clash with the enemy throughout Kontum and Pleiku Provinces.[32/]

On 11/12 April FSB Charlie came under heavy attack, but the ARVN 11th Airborne Bn, aided by the timely arrival of TACAIR, repelled the enemy with 200 KIA.[33/] This incident signalled the beginning of a coordinated enemy effort, and artillery and ground attacks occurred in many different locations. The Ben Het Ranger Camp west of Dak To was attacked as were FSB's Six, Zulu, and Yankee (YB991130). The enemy employed 130mm artillery for the first time in the campaign in the attack on FSB Yankee.[34/]

In the Eastern sector of MR II, clashes occurred at the An Khe pass on QL19. Here ARVN and Republic of Korea (ROK) forces clashed with two enemy battalions attempting to interdict the vital supply route between Qui Nhon and Pleiku cities. During the period 12/13 April Qui Nhon City received a ground and sapper attack and was cut off from QL 1: 7x122mm rockets hit Cam Ranh Bay, and 4x107mm rounds hit Nha Trang.[35/]

One of the enemy's objectives seemed to center on the interdiction of major road arteries from the coast to the Central Highlands, and between

Pleiku and Kontum cities, to deny the use of these routes for ARVN's resupply, replacement and redeployment.

Loss of FSB Charlie

The intensity of the action in the highlands increased daily. Heavy contacts between ARVN and the enemy took place north of Phung Hoang Air Base. Kontum City airport was rocketed, and on 14/15 April FSB Charlie was abandoned by its defenders, who had not been supplied in four days.[36/] The withdrawal by the ARVN airborne unit defenders was orderly, and had cost the NVA 48th Regiment so dearly that it was forced to move out of the line to refit and replace heavy losses.[37/] In contrast to the ignominious defeat yet to come at Tan Canh/Dak To, the ARVN Rangers acquitted themselves admirably. In a contemporary newspaper interview a U.S. Army FAC stated that[38/]

> *both sides showed a lot of guts. . . . The people on Charlie were far outnumbered, but they held on. . . . They never did break. They made the reds take bunker by bunker. They just did not give up and run. And the NVA, even though they lost as many as 800 kept coming. Both sides showed a lot of guts. . . . Wave after wave of TACAIR pounded them. . . . Cobras, F-4's, A-7, A-37 . . . even after ARVN soldiers had evacuated the base camp. Air strikes made the base and road adjacent to it a wasteland. If what they wanted was an infiltration route, they've got it, but if they want the ridge northwest of Kontum the big stuff is yet to come, and if they try to hit another of those base camps, it'll take them a long time to regroup afterwards.*

ARVN forces and air strikes continued to take their toll of the enemy. POWs stated that some of their battalions had lost up to one third of their manpower on the infiltration route from NVN. Most of this personnel attrition was ascribed to air strikes.[39]

The continuing closure of QL19 from Qui Nhon to Pleiku cities began to cause supply problems in the Central Highlands. Lt General Dzu, ARVN Commander of MR II, restricted the expenditure of artillery ammunition in Kontum Province. Soon other supplies would reach critical proportions. Rice reserves in Kontum City had fallen from 700 to 19 tons by 19 April.[40]

Enemy Objectives

Enemy objectives were not limited to the purely military aims of interdiction but included political and psychological goals as well. By engagement of the usually inferior PF/RF militia units the enemy hoped to weaken, discredit, and destroy the concepts of Vietnamization and Pacification. This, coupled with the military victories he hoped to achieve, would be a clear signal to the Americans at the Paris talks to abandon RVN and agree to terms. Or so the enemy hoped.

The immediate enemy objectives in the highlands were best summarized by a POW from the 400th Sapper Regiment, B-3 Front, who claimed that Phase I of the campaign "Truong Song Chuyen Minh" (The Western Mountains Rise Up) was designed to destroy ARVN military bases, stores, and equipment in the Tan Canh area, as well as to open routes for enemy movement. This phase was to last from February through April. Phase II envisioned the occupation of Ben Het, Dak To, Tan Canh FSB Six, and key points along Route 14 preparatory to an attack on Kontum City.[41/]

The Enemy Offensive Continues

Scattered incidents occurred in Pleiku and Kontum Provinces for several days after the fall of FSB Charlie. In Binh Dinh Province ROK and ARVN units, supported by U.S. and VNAF air, attempted to reopen the An Khe pass, but it remained closed to friendly traffic. Tam Quan and Hoai An district capitals in this east coast province fell to the enemy by 20 April.

Increased sensor-detected logistics activity in Base Area 609 signaled major enemy moves in the Central Highlands. A heavy ABF of 300-400 mixed rounds pounded the Dak Pek Ranger Camp on 19/20 April. Enemy losses during subsequent ground attack were put at 130 KIA to four friendlies KIA.[42/] Stinger 12, an AC-119 gunship supporting friendlies during the attack on this camp, noted in the Gunship Operational Summary that:[43/]

> *ASAP launch, worked with Uranium 99, who said Vietnamese Commander in target area at Dak Pek estimated between 60 to 80 VC casualties KBA.*

The following day ABFs occurred at FSB's Bravo, Delta, Hotel and Yankee. A wartime twist of fate felled the enemy, when[44/]

> *one enemy force opened up on the nearby camps of Bravo and Hotel and fifteen minutes later B-52 strikes rained down on them. The boxes had been preplanned for that day, but the almost unbelievable timing cost the enemy his initiative. All firing stopped abruptly after the air strikes.*

Dak Pek Ranger Camp continued under fire, as did the FSBs and Dak To. Stingers (AC-119s) and Spectres (AC-130s) supporting friendlies in these actions reported heavy AAA in the area. Such reports coincided with enemy plans as gleaned from prisoner interrogations. A U.S. intelligence source reported that [45/]

> *two NVA POWs captured in Kontum Province state that the NVA 2nd Division plans an attack on Hill 923, south of Dak To, to acquire high ground for the AAA site to protect 4 Bn of tanks and artillery arriving from Laos. Latter are to join the 2nd Division in a major assault on Tan Canh, 3 km west of Dak To. This attack is designed to complement attacks by the 320th NVA division along Rocket Ridge (this may have begun 21 April with the action at FSB Delta). NVA effort to take Hill 923 delayed on 20 April by word that tanks and artillery arrivals behind schedule. POWs speculate 24/25 will see beginning of action.*

On 21 April FSB Delta received a heavy mortar and artillery barrage; this was followed by a ground attack supported by three tanks. The defenders withdrew 500 meters to FSB Delta South.[46/] Spectre 08 reported that Stinger 02 was giving support to the defenders as they withdrew south. Spectre 08 further reported that "we have possible tanks 200 meters south of the fire base. Open fire and score 1 hit."[47/] All three tanks were knocked out by defenders before they withdrew.[48/]

Tanks at Tan Canh/Dak To

Enemy activity begun on the morning of 23 April was designed to destroy Tan Canh, the HQ of the ARVN 22d Division. The enemy launched artillery, mortar and sapper attacks; his tanks were reported in the vicinity of Dak To, north of Phung Hoang airport and east of FSB Delta. The enemy also

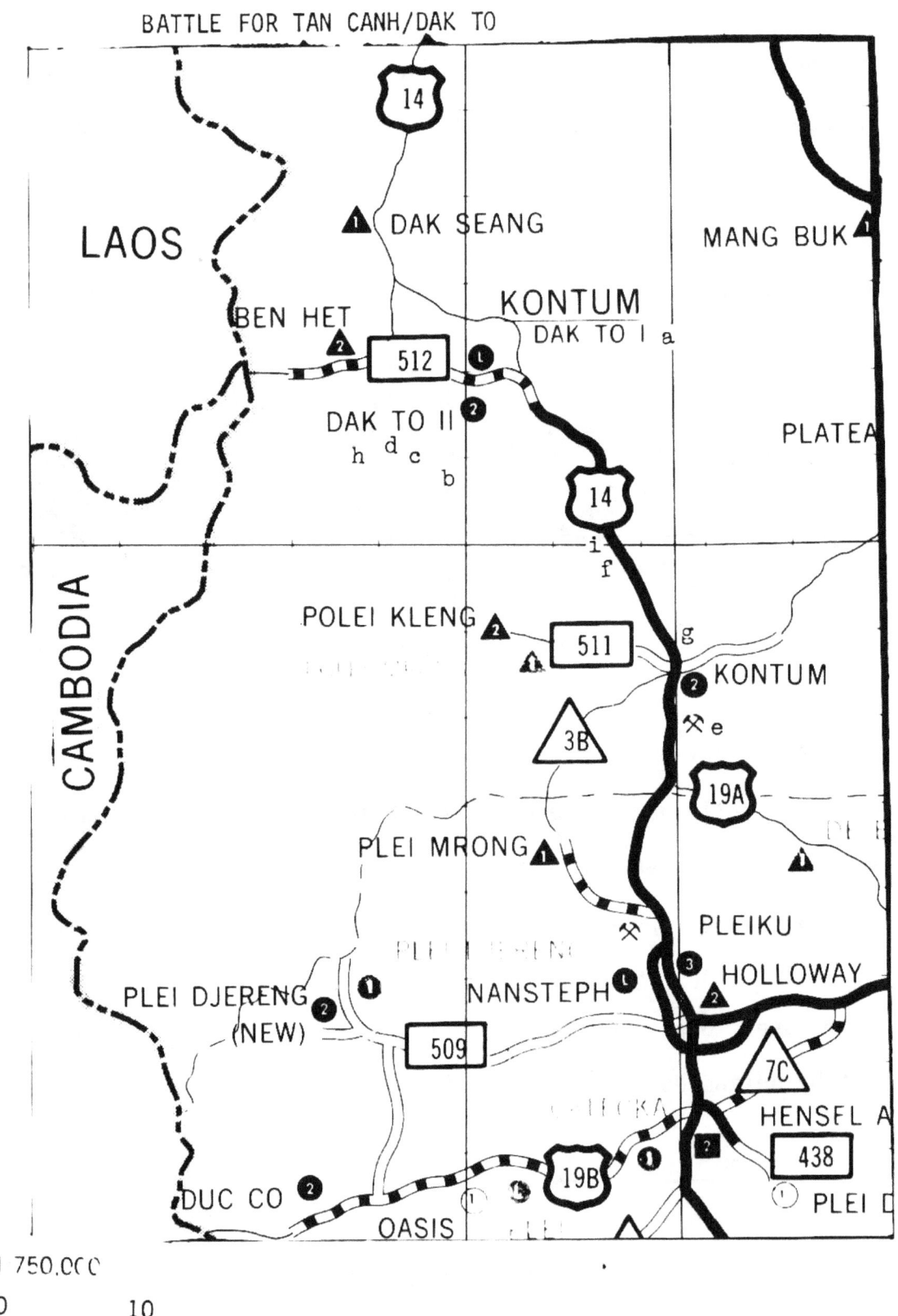

Scale 1:750,000

a. Tan Canh
b. Rocket Ridge
c. FSB 5
d. FSB 6
e. "Rockpile"
f. Vo Dinh
g. FSB November
i. FSB Charlie
j. FSB Delta South

FIGURE 2

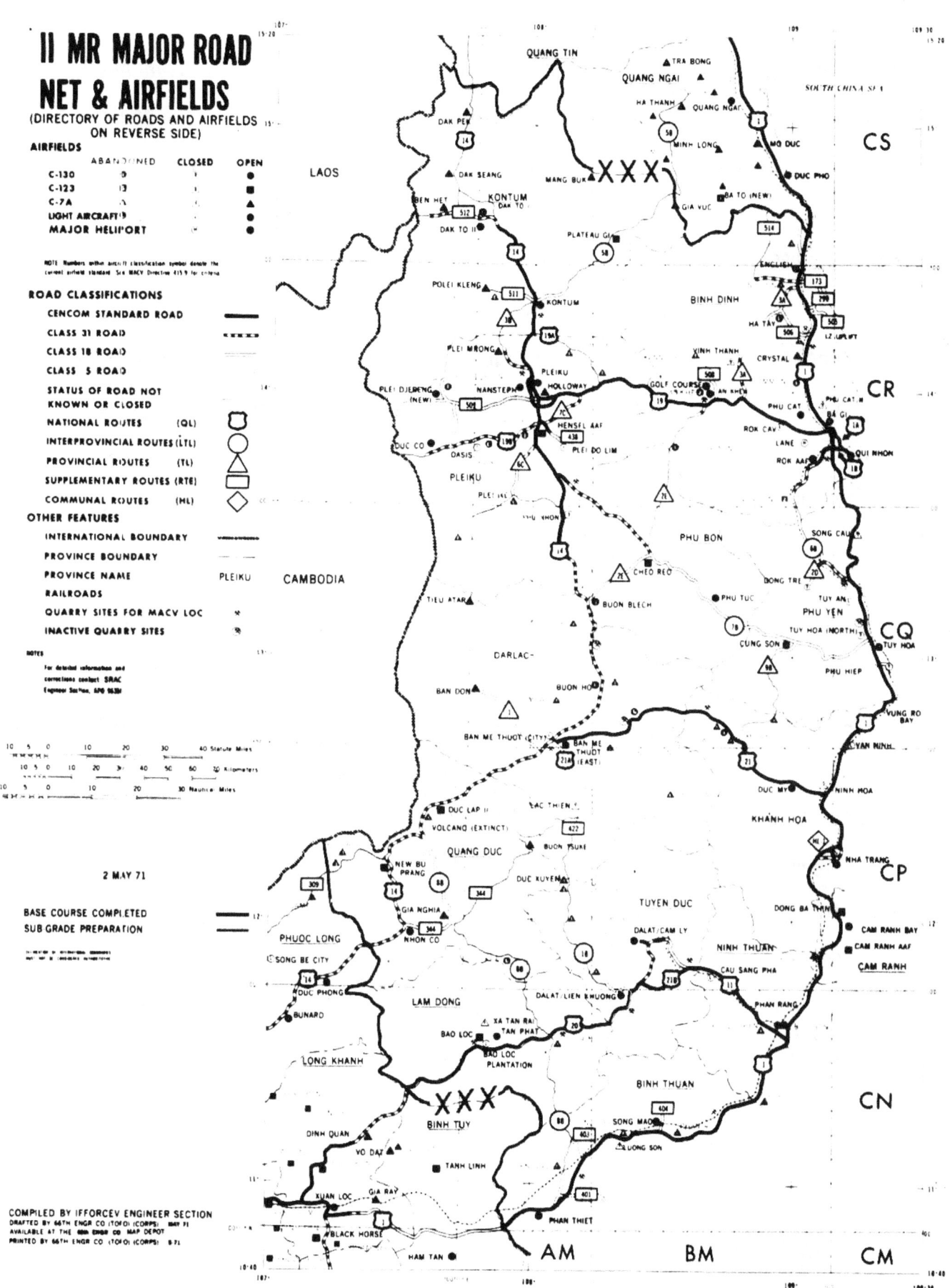

FIGURE 3

introduced his own wire-guided missiles (WGMs) and destroyed an ARVN M-41 tank with one at the gate of Tan Canh. Six more WGMs hit the 22d Division Forward Tactical Operations Center (TOC) wounding 50, including two U.S. advisors. FACs working in the area confirmed the presence of one 122mm and two 130mm guns.[49] Air support to the Tan Canh/Dak To region rapidly increased when a tactical emergency (TAC-E) was declared in the area.[50] Nevertheless the situation continued to deteriorate when enemy forces cut QL14 in three places above Dak To and south of Tan Canh. Route 14 was also cut south of Kontum City at the Chu Pao Pass, which became known as the "Rockpile." The Tan Canh/Dak To area was now effectively cut from Kontum City, and Kontum City was isolated from Pleiku City.[51]

Now positive sightings of tanks and other vehicles increased in the Tan Canh area. At 1930H, 23 April 1972, Second Regional Assistance Group (SRAG) TOC reported ABFs at Tan Canh, FSB Delta South, FSB 41, Polei Kleng, FSB 5, and Vo Dinh. Dak To District HQ reported up to 30 vehicles moving south. By 2310H a 22d Division forward element identified the vehicles as tanks moving south on QL14 toward Tan Canh;[52] a PAVE AEGIS (105mm howitzer equipped) Spectre gunship, on-station and engaging the tanks, reported a positive 10 tanks identified, and a probable 20-22 vehicle total. A subsequent report credited the Spectre (probably Spectre 19) with taking the tanks under fire; reportedly destroying one and damaging four.[53]

Spectre 11, piloted by Captain Russel T. Olson, was fragged to Tan Canh/Dak To on a fire support mission the same evening. Arriving in the beleaguered area, the gunship's crew found hostile T-54 tanks approaching friendly positions. Spectre 11 immediately engaged the tanks, although encountering 23mm and 51 caliber AAA fire, and dispersed the massed concentration. Unable to obtain a replacement aircraft, Spectre 11 made a rapid turn-around at Pleiku Air Base, and returned to the Tan Canh/Dak To area as dawn broke on the battlefield. A thick cloud layer obscured the battle area, and Spectre 11 chose to descend below its minimum normal daylight working altitude to support friendly ground personnel. In doing so, it exposed itself to 57mm,* and the more usual AAA fire. Spectre 11 drew the fire from two of the tanks onto itself, and away from 11 United States Army advisory personnel who were being heli-lifted out of the area. Though running low on fuel, Spectre 11 remained to act as a FAC for newly-arrived TACAIR, which could not locate the targets independently due to low clouds, smoke and haze. Only after seeing the rescue operation to its successful conclusion did Spectre 11 leave the area. Although BDA assessment was difficult under the chaotic conditions of the battlefield, HQ 7AF confirmed that a minimum of seven enemy tanks were rendered useless by the gunship.[54/] The performance of the PAVE AEGIS gunships so impressed the ground troops that whenever Spectres appeared on the scene subsequently they were asked if they had "the big gun."[55/]

*This was undoubtedly from the ZSU57/2, a T-54 body with twin 57mm AAA and target acquisition equipment. Usually the enemy used it like a normal tank instead of in its AAA role.

In spite of the efforts of PAVE AEGIS, the remaining tanks continued toward Tan Canh at a high rate of speed. Four additional tanks were reported destroyed by the Vietnamese north of Tan Canh, but the remaining force entered Tan Canh Village at 0130H, 24 May. Artillery called in on the remaining tanks destroyed two to three more vehicles, but by dawn the remainder of the enemy tank force had surrounded Tan Canh. Three tanks had entered the Command Post (CP) compound virtually unopposed by elements of the ARVN 22d Division, who waited in their bunkers.[56/] Not all ARVN troops remained inactive. Elements of the 47th Regiment at Vo Dinh attempted to negotiate three enemy road interdictions to link up with elements of the 9th Airborne Battalion in the Dak To area.[57/] Heavy 23mm AAA fire and closing weather inhibited air support, although "the Dak To area was critical and supported with maximum TACAIR and gunships."[58/]

Having overrun Tan Canh, the tanks quickly turned west. By 1430H Dak To II was firmly under their control. All battalions of the 42d and 47th Regiments plus 1/41st Bn were fragmented and no longer considered combat effective in the area. A defensive line ordered around Vo Dinh consisted of five Ranger and one Airborne Bn, plus all the 22d Division stragglers moving south. Troops at FSBs Delta South and Hotel moved to FSB Metro, while FSB 5 and 6 forces moved to the Ben Het Ranger Camp. The 9th Airborne Bn moved from the Dak To II area south to Vo Dinh. No friendly troops were left on Rocket Ridge. U.S. casualties among 22d Division advisory personnel were four KIA, one WIA and 10 Missing in Action (MIA), the latter figure due to a helicopter crash near Dak To on the 24th.[59/]

Why Did Tan Canh/Dak To Fall?

Many individuals associated with ARVN speculated on the failure to hold Tan Canh/Dak To. A FAC flying near Tan Canh shortly before the battle recalled that [60]

> *the day before Tan Canh, I noticed a lot of trucks on old QL14 north of Tan Canh. It had hardly ever received any use. . . . I called up II DASC requesting air for these. Of course no air was available because of other priority targets. . . . the next day the tanks showed up at Tan Canh.*

While this may be cited as a possible factor, one must remember that continuous air coverage began as soon as tanks were sighted on 23 April. Only the poor weather conditions on the morning of the 24th prevented full and effective use of aircraft, particularly the "fast movers." A senior U.S. Army advisor put it in these terms: [61]

> *Prior to the Tan Canh battle we felt we weren't getting our fair share of air, but once they started moving additional support units in I think we faired pretty well. Right now we're getting about 100 sorties per day, which is pretty damn good!*

In a different vein, he added: [62]

> *We taught them (the South Vietnamese) some bad habits with the fire Support Base Concept. These are little islands in the middle of no place using bunkers as command posts and bunkers for sleeping, and when the enemy is ready to knock out these islands all he has to do is put a devastating amount of indirect fire and everything collapses.*

A new USAF advisor to the South Vietnamese ventured in his opinion that [63/]

> they [ARVN] were not trained specifically to handle a conventional war. They were trained for guerrilla warfare, because that's the only kind of warfare we had in the past.

However a veteran senior U.S. advisor to the 23d ARVN Division disagreed, and he stated that [64/]

> we trained them both ways, but we tried not to burden them with large bulky equipment so they could also fight the counter-guerrilla war. I think the reason they broke and ran initially was the surprise of the tanks. They had never fought tanks before. They had plenty of anti-tank devices,* but no one could visualize a bunch of T-54s and T-59s. . . . The best units when completely surprised might run and break.

It appeared that the ARVN 22d Division could not be counted among "the best units." One novice USAF advisor suggested that the caliber of the enlisted men was below average and that the unit was "poorly led." [65/] There were other explanations ventured, but all agreed that the main problem was psychological. A senior SRAG officer commented that [66/]

> ARVN was psyched by tanks. They didn't have a good psychological program to counter the tank threat. . . . They think the NVA is 9 feet tall, and he's not. He's a basic Vietnamese, and he thinks and acts like a Vietnamese; except I suspect he's probably better led.

*Among them the M-72 Light Anti-Tank Weapon (LAW) used very successfully at Kontum City in May.

A segment of the unprecedented NVA invasion, using every weapon in its arsenal and almost every man it could muster, rolled over ARVN forces in the first major encounter in the Central Highlands. The reasons are many, and all are valid to some degree, i.e.: the firebases did not hold out as long as expected; increasing cloud cover hindered the optimum use of airpower; ARVN leadership was poor, as were some of the troops; and the psychological effect of tanks and 130mm guns broke the will to resist. Further, the high casualty rate following the missile attack on the 22d Division TOC on 23 April undoubtedly lowered the morale of officers and enlisted men alike.

Developments Through 30 April 1972

One could not cite material problems for ARVN's failure to counter the NVA threat at Tan Canh/Dak To. Loss figures revealed that retreating 22d Division troops left the enemy 23x105mm howitzers; 7x155mm field pieces, 10 M-41 tanks, and 16,000 rounds of ammunition (primarily 105mm).[67/] This unfortunate scene was repeated several times, and not only in MR II. The Senior Fighter Duty Officer at III DASC commented that on[68/]

> *the first two weeks of this offensive we used at least 80% of our TACAIR destroying our own stuff which ARVN left when they broke and ran. That's my major complaint about ARVN; if you've got to retreat at least blow up your equipment.*

It would be unfair and untrue to assert that all ARVN units were ineffective. Certainly the Ranger and Airborne battalions near Tan Canh/ Dak To put up a spirited defense, as did some elements of the ill-fated

22d Division. Remnants of these units filtered initially toward Vo Dinh to regroup, but later were absorbed into the ARVN 23d Division. Many proved their determination in the battles for Kontum City.

Palace circles in Saigon were reported upset with the defeat of the ARVN 22d Division and tended to blame the division commander and Lt General Dzu. The loss of the northern approaches to Kontum City was termed "unnecessary," especially since Dzu had assured Saigon that he could hold them. 69/ General Dzu's days as commander were numbered. One officer at II DASC recalled that 70/

> *General Dzu, the previous Commander, was a sorry figure. After Tan Canh fell, and when he should have been out trying to rally his troops, he was coming in to us all the time saying give us max TACAIR. He wanted to blow up everything, villages, everything. He was damn near in a state of panic.*

Indeed, ominous days were ahead for the forces in MR II. After overrunning Tan Canh/Dak To, enemy units continued south toward Kontum City. The city, cut off by units of the NVA 95B Regiment to the south (at the "Rockpile"), was now in danger of being isolated from the north. Again, airpower provided the ARVN 23d Division with the priceless time needed to set up hastily developed defenses. Gunships, TACAIR and B-52s pounded the enemy every step of the way, and it was not uncommon to read mission reports such as the following two extracts: 71/

> *Visually found two trucks . . . damaged one with a hit with 105mm and lost the other truck in the foliage. . . . Covey 518 found 4 trucks for us, all of which we destroyed.*
>
> *Cleared to work west of Dak To for trucks and tanks. When we called in BDA we estimated 12-16 destroyed and 12 damaged.*

FACs guided F-4s and other fast movers into the Tan Canh area to destroy the war material ARVN had abandoned. The supersonic fighter-bombers, using the new Laser Guided Bombs (LGBs) also became tank killers, and were often guided on-target by Spectre gunships.[72/] On 26 April, U.S. TACAIR using guided and unguided bombs destroyed a vital bridge on QL14 near Dien Bien. Enemy armor, rolling south toward Kontum City, was effectively, although temporarily, halted at that point. Continuous TACAIR and gunship coverage of the area prevented repairs to the structure.[73/]

Heavy AAA posed a severe threat to the extensive air cover employed. The crew of Spectre 10 stated that in the Dak To area they[74/]

> *had to break off target due to AAA on a nearby hill and AAA associated radar. This occurred during the day VFR to the SQ of Dak To. Recommend AC-130s not work during daylight hours due to the AAA threat in this area. . . . AAA radar and 37mm have been moved into this area. Possible 57mm in this area associated with AAA radar. It was very hard to break AAA radar lock-on. Spectre 07 worked this same area and had not encountered AAA during hours of darkness.*

Through all odds, the application of air assets slowed the enemy Blitzkrieg. Why the enemy suddenly became cautious after the lightning

Air Force Fighter/Bombers Destroy Tank at Dak To

FIGURE 4

Spectre Destroys Trucks on Route 14

FIGURE 5

victory at Tan Canh is a moot question, but one senior advisor commenting on the devastating effects of airpower said, "After the fall of Tan Canh, the enemy lost approximately 40% of his forces on his drive on Kontum City." 75/ Another U.S. advisor added: 76/

> *In fact, I know the enemy was surprised beyond his wildest dreams that he took Tan Canh as quickly as he did. If he had been able to exploit that success, he could have been in Kontum that afternoon or the next day, but it was beyond his capabilities. His supply lines were extended - plus he didn't have the rationale - conventional warfare is new to him as well.*

Continued losses slowed the enemy, but did not stop him; and widely scattered actions continued throughout the highlands. Kontum and Pleiku cities were not spared during and after the drive on Tan Canh, and both received several ABFs. On 22 April, for example, an Air Vietnam plane was hit by enemy fire while on the ground at Kontum City airport. A stewardess was killed and several passengers were wounded. The aircraft was 80 percent damaged. 77/ On the 26th, the Ben Het Ranger Camp took some 400-500 rounds of mixed fire. This was followed early on the morning of the 27th by a ground attack, which was once again repulsed by the Montagnard defenders. Some 400 ARVN troops from the 22d Division, who had fled to Ben Het from Tan Canh, were heli-lifted out of Ben Het on the 26th. Other units of this division were sent to Pleiku City for reorganization. 78/

The news from eastern MR II was mixed. Negatively, all of Binh Dinh Province seemed in danger of falling; on the positive side, ROK and ARVN troops reopened the An Khe Pass on 26 April. By 1600H a food convoy traveled through the pass without incident. The reopening of highway 19 eased the resupply of the Central Highlands. The Bong Son Pass on Route 1 was also reported cleared, although the enemy was still located in the high ground above the pass. Once again, the role of airpower in the pass clearing operation was significant and 7AF reported that "heavy U.S. TACAIR and B-52 strikes in the area over the past few days were decisive in helping clear the enemy from the target." 79/ In the Central Highlands, efforts to reopen the QL14 pass at the "Rockpile" continued to be inconclusive; although massive ARC LIGHT and TACAIR strikes supported the ARVN 45th Regiment in the operation.

Enemy ABFs continued throughout the highlands at Dak Pek, FSB Echo, Radar Site Peacock (near Pleiku City), and at Kontum City itself. The situation looked very grim as April drew to a close. Rocket Ridge had been lost, and Vo Dinh was abandoned on 29 April. 80/ The 23d Division slowly began to organize the defense of Kontum City along conventional lines. A CAS report stated that 81/

> *the situation in Kontum appears to be deteriorating; senior officials believe the city can't hold out 24 hours if attacked soon. However, they say if the attack can be stalled one week the organized defenses may be able to hold the city.*
>
> *Morale in Pleiku is bad with rumors that Lt General Dzu is to be replaced. All non essential U.S. military personnel evacuated from Kontum and Pleiku. President Thieu ordered the families of military members out of Kontum and Pleiku Provinces. Air tickets to Saigon, normally 2850P ($7) are black marketed for 10,000 Piasters.*

Once again, airpower provided the precious time. The last news on 30 April proved a ray of hope when it was reported that[82/]

> *an ARC LIGHT strike at 1790H on 30 April west of FSB Lima evidently frustrated plans by the 64th and 48th Regiments of the 320th Division to attack Lima. At least 50 KBA were reported by helicopters on a BDA mission following the strike. Additionally, 40-50 personnel in a dazed condition were observed 10 minutes after the strike and were engaged by the gunships involved in the BDA mission.*

This action took place only 15 km northwest of Kontum City.

CHAPTER III

MAY 1972: THE ASSAULTS ON KONTUM CITY

Function of the II DASC

"MR II was supposed to be completely Vietnamized by June, and the II DASC, where I work, was supposed to close then. That was before the current offensive, of course."[83/] Thus spoke one of the handful of United States Air Force (USAF) personnel at the Direct Air Support Center,* Pleiku City.

The II DASC included USAF and VNAF personnel, with the Americans acting primarily as advisors. During the offensive, U.S. personnel became more active in advising the U.S. Army SRAG at MR II HQs on the proper employment of tactical airpower in joint air/ground operations, and in providing control and direction of tactical airpower used in support of requests from ARVN. The Senior Fighter Duty Officer at II DASC put it this way:[84/]

> *TACAIR is used with FACs. The FACs go out and look for targets, or the ground commander will direct them to a target or give them an area to check out. He calls back here with the coordinates to be cleared, and also requests air at the same time. We clear the target here by going through ARVN channels. After that's done, we have our incoming air that's been fragged to us; we parcel it out to the FAC depending on what priority target he's got. Number one priority, of course, is anyone who's got a tactical emergency-*

---

*For a more extensive report on II DASC checo CHECO report #20-188, <u>The DASC's in II Corps Tactical Zone July 1965-June 1969</u>. This report is classified SECRET.

> *like if they're being overrun. The second is troops
> in contact; next in line is troops in the open etc.*

The same source, in explaining B-52 targeting said somewhat tongue-in-cheek: 85/

> *Frankly, that's no longer an Air Force weapon. We
> fly the airplane, but the (U.S.) Army puts in the
> target request; they handle the clearing etc. The
> only thing we do is hand out the air strike warning
> to our own aircraft, so they won't have bombs
> dumped on them.*

The Offensive Continues

When B-52 raids slowed the enemy's move south, and broke his attack on FSB Lima, USAF sources at II DASC reported that 86/

> *Mr. Vann this morning expressed his great appreciation
> for the role currently effected by U.S. TACAIR and ARC
> LIGHT missions. He feels that the ARC LIGHTs in partic-
> ular have severely hurt the enemy, and that this com-
> bined with TACAIR has stalled the enemy in mounting
> their expected offensive at Kontum. Intercepted enemy
> radio traffic reports that quote bombs continue to fall
> on us and we cannot attack unquote.*

The situation at Kontum City remained static, but an attack was expected in the near future. Mr. Vann expressed his confidence in ARVN's ability to hold Kontum. 87/ Such ability was called into question again when ARVN forces walked off and abandoned FSB Lima at 1800H, 1 May. They left numerous trucks, tanks, artillery pieces and other equipment behind, and made no attempt to destroy them. At this point II Corps then requested TACAIR to destroy this FSB and the abandoned equipment. This was accomplished as requested.[88/] The situation at the QL 14 "Rockpile" remained stalemated, particularly when bad weather precluded many airstrikes in the area. Use of Cluster Bomb Units (CBU)-55 on this target proved highly successful, but ARVN would not take follow-up action.[89/] The II DASC noted that[90/]

> *II Corps is still apparently relying totally on TACAIR and ARC LIGHT support for offensive operations in this AO. This support is still considered outstanding both in quality and quantity.*

With the loss of the FSBs, SRAG attempted to replace the lost ground positions with a Command and Control (CC) helicopter. The senior USAF representatives at II DASC disagreed with the plan, since it tended to usurp II DASC's TACAIR support responsibility, and required two additional Air Liaison Officers (ALOs). He felt that[91/]

> *FAC and Spectre support remains outstanding, and in addition to their basic mission, they are practically the sole source of accurate recon/intelligence information in the immediate area of tactical operations.*

News from the east coast continued to be bad. Early on 3 May some 2000 friendly troops abandoned Landing Zone (LZ) English, and again left all their useable equipment behind. U.S. and VNAF TACAIR were once again called on to deny this material to the enemy. Air and Naval gunfire supported the evacuation of these men by U.S. Navy landing craft.[92/]

In the highlands the situation became more critical when Polei Kleng and Ben Het received ABFs, and enemy artillery began to zero-in on Kontum

City. Next, the South Vietnamese Joint General Staff (JGS) ordered the airborne unit out of Kontum and back to Saigon. The loss of these 1000-1500 sorely needed troops at this juncture caused much despair at II Corps, particularly since a planned combat assault on the QL 14 "Rockpile" was to take place within a few days. Air support remained a bright spot: 93/

> *Covey, Rustic and Nail FACs, as well as Spectre and Stinger gunships remain in high demand by this MR. . . . Mr. Vann continues to laud their contribution to the effort.*

Also encouraging were the reports of a new "air" weapon, helicopter mounted and issued to the U.S. Air Cavalry. This was the Tube Launched, Optically Tracked, Wire Guided Missile (TOW), which was to be used so successfully at the upcoming battles of Kontum City. Plans were made to use this weapon in conjunction with Spectres, when Spectres were using only their 40mm. 94/

The "Rockpile" Operation

The ARVN-conceived assaults on the Chu Pao Pass commenced on 4 April. USAF TACAIR met its commitment and prepared the LZ for the ARVN troop drop. However, the ARVN insertion came some four hours behind schedule due to poor coordination with VNAF helicopter forces. A similar situation on the following day caused the senior USAF representative at II DASC to point out the poor VNAF helicopter support to General Vogt, Commander 7AF. He said that "the failure to insert reinforcements into this operation could mean the difference between success and failure." 95/ The ARVN 45th Regiment moved up Route 14 from Pleiku City, while the 2d Ranger Battalion moved south from Kontum City. Indeed, on 5 May both units went through the pass, but any thoughts of vicoty in the operation proved illusory. By 6 May the pass was closed again, and would remain so for many weeks despite continued air-supported ARVN attempts to reopen it.[96/] When the senior USAF representative at II DASC heard that ARVN was considering abandoning the effort after only a few days, due to "lack of support," he countered: "If this is true, it is because they are reluctant to engage the enemy - air support seemed adequate. No BDA can be reliably obtained from this operation. . . ."[97/]

Closing in on Kontum City

At 1515H, 5 May, a USAF FAC confirmed five tanks and enemy troops moving toward Polei Kleng. Early that evening the situation became grave when the enemy tanks and troops arrived at the compound wire, but TACAIR with MR-82s, Rockeyes, and LGBs responded to the TAC "E", as did Spectre gunships. Once again, air repelled what might have been an almost certain enemy overrun of the camp. Twelve sorties were flown in support of the TAC "E" with one AAA pit and a possible two tanks damaged. Nightfall, smoke and foliage prevented accurate BDA. The remainder of the sorties that night were dropped by COMBAT SKYSPOT on targets northwest of Kontum City.[98/]

Although repulsed at the wire, the enemy continued to pound Polei Kleng with 130mm artillery fire. The ARVN Ranger Battalion was reported in "gross disorder" after the CP area had taken several hits. By 1930H on the 6th, three U.S. advisors at the camp were heli-lifted to Pleiku, although the Rangers were still tenuously holding the site.

Meanwhile, tanks and troops were reported moving on the Ben Het Ranger Camp, and a Spectre moved in to suppress the activity. Dak Pek, Dak Seang, and Plei Mrong also reported ABFs. The increased enemy action called forth expanded air support. TACAIR sorties to the highlands region went from almost nil on 1 May to 45 on the night of 6 May. This figure included USAF, United States Navy (USN) and the United States Marine Corps (USMC) aircraft.[99/] On 7 May the enemy hurled 160mm mortar shells at the Ben Het Ranger Camp, the first use of this weapon in MR II. Against the backdrop of increased activity Montagnard forces "revolted," wounding the ARVN camp commander.[100/] Rocket 82, the U.S. advisor, reported that the Montagnard Rangers had demanded withdrawal from the threatened FSB within 48 hours. Apparently they wanted to be relocated with their families, whom they had not seen for two months. The "revolt" continued to simmer, but constant enemy pressure on the camp forced the Montagnards to concentrate their efforts elsewhere. The II DASC reported that the "Ben Het revolt is still current, but quiet at this time, and they are fighting well. Could be we need more revolts."[101/] The II Corps Commander agreed to move the Montagnards out as soon as air extraction became possible.[102/]

Enemy activity in the general area around Kontum continued to intensity, presaging the attack on the city itself. Polei Kleng had another TAC "E" at 0800H, 8 May, and VNAF TACAIR responded with A-37 and A-1 support. USAF and VNAF FACs continued to work the area, although the weather precluded maximum air support. Spectres and F-4s saved the day for Plei Mrong, which came under attack again.[103/] FSB 41, north of Pleiku, had been abandoned by the RF company holding it on 7 May; but it had been

retaken by ARVN elements on 8 May. On the following day, Polei Kleng received
another ground attack at 0500H, and evacuation began two hours later.
Poor weather conditions prevented TACAIR aid for the camp until 1100H,
but by that time all friendlies had departed. TACAIR then turned on enemy
troops and LOCs in the area. The early morning hours also brought a renewed
tank assault and TAC "E" at Ben Het. Spectres, and M-72 LAWs used by ground
troops, destroyed four PT-76 tanks. Several TACAIR sorties, both U.S.
and VNAF, claimed three more tanks destroyed and one damaged. The attack
was repulsed, even though the enemy held one-third of the compound at one
point. The attempt to extract the 71st Ranger Bn from Ben Het failed due
to heavy AAA surrounding the site. Although the enemy continued to mount
probes at Ben Het, they were held at bay by flares and fire from Spectre
gunships.104/ The seige continued during the following day. POWs reported
that the all-out assault on Ben Het was planned for that night. As a result,
II DASC requested priority on TACAIR and gunships. VNAF air drops to
beleaguered Ben Het landed outside the perimeter and supplies the enemy.
TACAIR continued to blow up supplies at the abandoned Polei Kleng camp,
and to punish the enemy buildup around Plei Mrong. The area immediately
around Kontum City was carefully watched by USAF FACs and U.S. Air Cavalry
for an attack on the provincial capital thought probable on Ho Chi Minh's
birthday, 19 May.105/ In the midst of the furious struggle Lt General Ngo
Dzu was replaced by Maj General Nguyen Van Toan as Commander of II Corps,
on 10 May. General Toan, the armored specialist on the JGS, was considered
tenacious in contrast to his predecessor.106/

The defense of Kontum City now rested with 11 regular ARVN battalions two RF Bns, 28 artillery pieces, and 10 tanks.[107/] A senior U.S. Army advisor recalled that[108/]

> *when we arrived, the 23d Division had not closed. In fact, it didn't close until the 13th of May - the day before the attack. It was the first time in war that the 23d Division had worked as a unit. After the battle of Tan Canh and the withdrawal of the 22d, we came into a group that was pretty well devastated moralewise.*

The situation in Pleiku and Kontum cities was deteriorating. Some 15,000 refugees from the Dak To area swelled the population of Kontum City, which continued to be hit by sporadic ABFs. On 9 May an Air Vietnam DC-4 was rocketed as it landed at Pleiku airfield, and II DASC prepared to put Phase One of a four phase evacuation plan into effect on 11 May.[109/]

Maneuvering for the Attack

The senior USAF representative at II DASC reported on the 11th that all areas in MR II were quiet--so quiet that SRAG and II Corps officials were "uneasy." He added that ARC LIGHT and TACAIR strikes at Ben Het had resulted in 304 KIA, primarily KBA, with some 65 individual weapons, several crew-served weapons, and an additional five PT-76 tanks destroyed.* The expected attack on Kontum City had not materialized, but 20 USAF and 12 VNAF TACAIR strikes continued to pound the main infiltration routes to Kontum and Pleiku.[110/]

*Four Soviet "Sagger" Wire-Guided Anti-Tank Missiles were also captured at Ben Het.

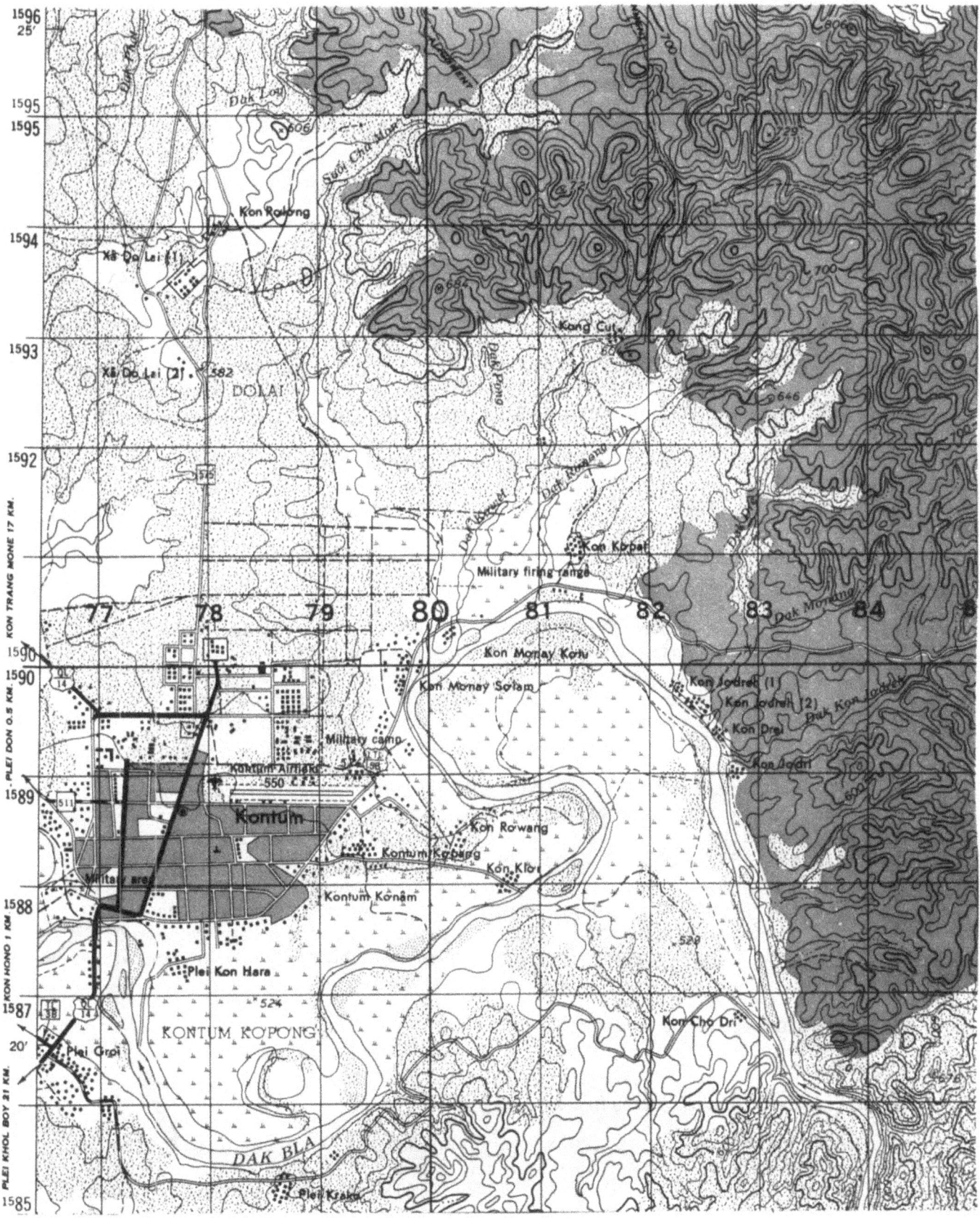

FIGURE 6

On the 12th, Pleiku airfield received 6x122mm rockets, and Kontum airfield took several rounds of incoming artillery, which hit very close to a C-130. Earlier, on 2 May, two other C-130s had been damaged by mortar and artillery fire. The incidents prompted 7AF to cease C-130 daylight operations into Kontum City on 12 May. The enemy had effectively zeroed-in on the Kontum runway, and the lack of effective return fire and probes from ARVN gave him free rein. SRAG and II Corps wanted the vital daylight resupply flights to continue, but the senior USAF representative at II DASC opted for night missions, provided all supply requirements could be met by them.[111/] The eve of the 13th presented a gloomy picture. As one senior U.S. advisor in Kontum City put it:[112/]

> *We had refugees by the tens of thousands . . . we kept on losing one FSB after another and the NVA kept on applying the pressure. However, from the time Tan Canh fell on 24 April to the battle at Kontum on the 14th we estimate that we killed about 40% of the NVA force - and it was predominantly with airpower. The tactic would be to hit the enemy as he was massing to attack the FSBs. From the assembly areas to the attack positions we would hit them, not only with tactical airpower but with ARC LIGHTS. We were really using the ARC LIGHTS as close-in protective fire; and as the enemy moved south they were used 1000 meters in front of the front lines as protective fire. We were having tremendous results with this firepower, but they kept on coming. The big question was, would the ARVN fight the tanks?*

That question would be answered shortly.

The First Attack on Kontum City

Increasing numbers of tanks and enemy troops were sighted in the area around Kontum City. U.S. and VNAF TACAIR attacked seven enemy tanks near Vo Dinh on the 13th with one tank reported destroyed. At Ben Het, VNAF helicopters attempted to extract some of the mutineers, but heavy AAA prevented success. Six VNAF A-1s were then assigned to provide protective cover, but failed to suppress enemy fire causing postponement of the operation. Failure dogged the QL 14 "Rockpile" clearing operation as well, and a route to the west, circumventing the pass, was examined as an alternative.[113/] The HQ of the NVA 2d Division was reported to be 15 km northwest of the city, with the HQ of the NVA 320th Division and 48th Regiment also in the area. This led most observers to feel that the show-down battle for Kontum City would take place within a few days.[114/]

The few days shortened to a few hours when ABFs and light ground probes occurred on the night of 13/14 May at FSB November, northwest of Kontum City, and at FSBs 41 and 42. By 0600H, an estimated 11 tanks and battalion-size infantry attacked Kontum City, primarily from the north and northwest. Would this be a repeat of Tan Canh? The 23d Division G-3 U.S. advisor on the scene recalled that[115/]

> *we found out on the 14th that they (ARVN) could fight the tanks. They fought the tanks before daylight, before we could bring in tactical air, the Cobras, the gunships, or the TOW missiles*

The ignominious defeat at Tan Canh was not repeated. ARVN 23d Division ground troops engaged the initial tank assault with M-72 LAWs, and by 0730H helicopter gunships mounting TOWs and U.S./VNAF TACAIR had joined the engagement. By noon, USAF FACs reported six tanks out of action, with three burning. Enemy ground attacks by elements of the NVA 320th Division were repulsed north and west of the city, as was a small probe from the south along the Dak Bla River. The ARVN 23d Division had closed successfully, and coordination among ARVN, VNAF and U.S. forces was at a high point. The senior USAF officer at II DASC recalled:[116/]

> At one time today approx 1300H, TACAIR both VNAF and USAF was striking NE, NW and south of Kontum and friendly artillery firing to the west, all simultaneously. Mr. Vann, SRAG and USAF observers were on the scene, and Mr. Vann remarked that it was one of the greatest applications of power he had observed and he was elated. He was particularly impressed by VNAF performance and response. The ultimate occurred in coordination today when a VNAF FAC expended all his Willie Petes and a USAF FAC on the scene marked for the VNAF FAC using English language, and the VNAF FAC talked in the VNAF TACAIR using USAF FAC mark and accomplished a very successful air strike. . . . The operation at Kontum today was an all Vietnamese show, with VNAF and ARVN performing well. USAF and U.S. Army assisted only in a minor way. USAF TACAIR . . . was always ready to come in, if needed. The new II Corps Commander and most of his staff were on the scene . . . it appears that a new image of II Corps is in the making with an excellent start considering today's performance.

The back of the initial enemy thrust was quickly broken. The senior U.S. advisor to the 23d Division credited[117/]

> the application of the tactical airstrikes, both USAF and VNAF, with preventing an NVA follow-through of the initial lodgement they had made in our positions. The application of the B-52 strikes during this initial attack on the 14th was stepped-up in the Kontum area over what it had been. The strategic strikes were committed principally in a tactical role in the immediate vicinity of Kontum.

An American intelligence source confirmed the success of airpower in thwarting the 14 May attack when it reported that[118/]

> *at least two hundred enemy bodies and 100 individual weapons were observed on the morning of 15 May in an area, 4 km NW of Kontum City, where B-52 strikes had been delivered on 14 May.*

By 0130H, 15 May, the attack had tapered off, although incoming artillery and mortar fire continued. At Kontum airfield an ABF ignited JP-4 fuel in the POL storage area. Two incidents occurred near Pleiku where attacks left a POL tank burning and destroyed an ammo dump.[119/] The loss from the sapper attacks on the Pleiku POL storage area and the ammunition dump were as follows:[120/]

> *330 tons total, consisting of 97 tons dynamite, 90,000 feet of det cord, 18,000 lb blocks of TNT, 90,000 105mm fuses and various amounts of 40mm and 57mm and smaller ammo. Sabotage on the POL tanks on 15 May resulted in loss of 150,000 gal of JP-4, one tank and the pumping station. The system is back in operation at this time.*

On the 15th limited military activity continued. By noon the 95th Ranger Bn had replaced the mutinous 71st Ranger Battalion at Ben Het. Enemy units continued to threaten the camp and VNAF TACAIR destroyed 20 out of 30 enemy sampans near the beleaguered outpost. Spectre 04 reported nine secondary explosions (SEX) and the possible destruction of a tank north of Kontum City. It was apparent that the enemy had suffered large losses during the Sunday attack, but ARVN stocks, especially of vital artillery ammunition, were down to 10 percent in some cases. It became evident that increased C-130 resupply missions into Kontum City would be requested.[121/]

The enemy continually probed for a weak spot in ARVN defenses. FSB 41 (ZA 196695) repelled a ground attack on the 16th with the help of TACAIR. Some 40 enemy KBA were reported. In Kontum City, incoming enemy artillery set two VNAF C-123 supply aircraft on fire. One was loaded with ammunition, and resultant explosions pitted the runway and forced its closure.[122/]

Although QL 14 between Kontum and Pleiku cities remained closed, some 14,000 refugees streamed into Pleiku City from the Kontum area. Some 75 percent of Pleiku City's normal population of 60,000 had left. Work on defenses in the city was going slowly, without a sense of urgency, and the city was quiet and orderly.[123/]

The "quiet" atmosphere was tragically shattered at Kontum City on the afternoon of 17 May. The 7th Air Force intelligence bulletin reported that[124/]

> *a U.S. C-130 was attempting to take off (while under fire at Kontum airfield) and failed to achieve take-off speed. The aircraft hit a building at the end of the runway and exploded, causing ammunition and POL fires in adjacent areas. Seven U.S. personnel were killed and two were wounded in the accident. 3,000 rounds of 105mm howitzer ammunition, the JP-4 pumping station and all the JP-4 fuel was destroyed.*

An operation advanced by the senior USAF representative in II Corps involved airfield cleanup teams to keep the runway, ramp and taxiways clear at all times. He charged the Kontum Province Chief with providing some 100 people for this team. Planning for future eventualities, the USAF representative also suggested that a suitable drop zone be located, secured, and prepared in the event resupply of Kontum City by paradrop became necessary. He recommended the river bed to the south as a likely area. He also remained dissatisfied with ARVN actions regarding silencing of the enemy artillery, which had the airfield zeroed-in. He advocated sending ARVN infantry recon teams out to locate and destroy a particularly troublesome 105mm howitzer, but again ran into ARVN "reluctance" to mount offensive operations. He noted: "Thus far the favorite actions that the ARVN keep falling back on is an ARC LIGHT in the suspected area followed by TACAIR."[125]

Air Frustrates a Major Enemy Assault

Various enemy incursions and ABFs continued, primarily at the FSBs near Kontum City. Dak Pek Border Ranger Camp and FSB 42 Alpha received heavy AFBs, while the ARVN 44th Regiment located NW of Kontum City was subjected to heavy ground assaults supported by tanks. TACAIR and helicopter gunships heavily supported ground units in these actions. It was at this crucial point that one of the vagaries of war overtook the enemy. As dawn broke on the 19th, USAF F-4s and helicopter gunships supporting the ARVN 44th Regiment forced the retreating enemy into a preplanned ARC

ARC LIGHT strike box. The senior U.S. advisor to the ARVN 23d Division recalled:[126/]

> The next strike by the NVA occurred on the night of the 18th, again from the northwest and again they had armor, however, in this attack their armor kind of held back, and did not reach the forward defense lines. However, the infantry did, and on this night they made three separate attempts to penetrate our positions. On this night we had planned and were employing our B-52 strikes about 6 km from our outer defense lines to as close as 1 km. The VC attack had made initial penetrations into our forward defense positions by 0500, and the division commander was just about to call for his artillery fire on his own position against the NVA infantry. At this particular spot we had a B-52 strike that was planned for 0530, running approximately 1 km parallel to the front. I suggested that he hold off firing on his own positions until the strike went in. The strike did go in on time, and the NVA attack stopped immediately. The NVA pulled out of their positions and started running, at which time the front-line troops were able to kill quite a few.

John Paul Vann noted that[127/]

> there are many indications that the enemy has planned a major assault on Kontum City, but that his timetable has been disrupted by preemptive bombardments. Further attempts to seize Kontum are expected.

Although BDA figures varied according to source, there was no doubt that TACAIR and B-52 strikes hurt the enemy and caused his loss of momentum. A CAS report stated that[128/]

> a variety of sources indicate that the enemy is preparing a major attack on Kontum City in the very near future, but there are reports also that they may be having difficulty getting set for it. A rallier from the K-2 Bn, NVA 28th Regiment said on 18 May that his unit was disrupted by heavy losses from a B-52 strike as his Bn was moving into attack position. . . . Info from this rallier supports POW statements that the 28th Regiment has suffered heavy casualties. A POW from the NVA 64th Regiment, 320th Division, said that this regiment

> *received 600 replacements during March, April and May, suggesting a very high casualty rate that is probably continuing.*

Preludes to the Final Effort

The C-130 operation into Kontum airfield resumed on the night of 18/19 May, although incoming artillery of various types and the high AAA threat made this run extremely dangerous. Landings were now at the pilot's discretion, and fixed wing aircraft traffic was restricted to the hours of darkness. When a C-130 received small arms fire while landing on the 20th, two subsequent C-130 bladder birds were diverted to Pleiku airfield. By 1720H, Kontum airfield had received 12x122mm rockets, three of which hit a VNAF C-123 on the ramp, destroying it. The saga of C-130 resupply missions during the crucial days of May remains one of the USAF's finest achievements, and deserved credit goes to the brave crews who flew these dangerous assignments against great odds. Some 17 C-130 resupply missions were flown on 19 May and 15 on the 20th.[129/]

The whole range of aircraft in the U.S. and VNAF armada prepared to meet any contingency. When Ben Het reported tracked vehicles, Spectres and TACAIR responded. When the offensive to reopen Kontum pass began on 19/20 May, John Paul Vann stated that[130/]

> *the preliminary bombardments to open the Kontum pass started on 19 May with 36 TACAIR strikes. TACAIR will continue . . . thru 21 May, when a ground attack will start. . . . Their assault will be supported by B-52 strikes, U.S. and VNAF TACAIR and air cavalry.*

With an attack becoming likely daily, military activity increased at Kontum airport. First, an aircraft accident closed the airport to C-130 resupply. Spare 622, a C-130, blew a tire and broke a hydraulic line while landing. This effectively terminated the night airlift, except for a C-130 bladder bird and a C-130 which carried parts for Spare 622.[131/] Unfortunately, by early morning of the 22nd Spare 622 became the target of enemy artillery fire. A hit on the number one engine caused a fuel leak, which subsequent enemy fire ignited. Apparent ARVN indifference allowed the plane to continue burning until a U.S. Army Colonel put out the blaze with a large fire extinguisher. However, the aircraft had to be considered a loss.[132/]

Next, at 0220H, 23 May, an enemy rocket hit the ramp of Kontum airport. A C-130 bladder bird, bringing in vitally needed fuel, took off immediately without unloading. When enemy action ceased shortly thereafter the runway reopened and some seven C-130s landed and unloaded on the night of 22/23 May.[133/]

C-130 resupply continued with a protective shield. Spectre gunships flew escort duties for the transport aircraft, and provided AAA suppression. Often the mere presence of a Spectre hovering over Kontum airfield proved effective enough to silence enemy guns and rockets.[134/] The ubiquity of air support was well expressed in the following fragment from the Daily Staff Journal kept in Kontum City:[135/]

> *23 May. Spectre 02 engaging truck . . . ARC LIGHT detonated NE of Kontum. Covey 564 on station Kontum . . . C-130 landed and unloaded . . . Covey 550 directing airstrikes on enemy.*

The time was fast approaching when all available assets would be required. Kontum airfield continued to receive occasional ABFs, but the runway remained open. The importance of the resupply mission could be ascertaine from John Paul Vann's description:[136/]

> *240204Z May 1972. Thirteen C-130 sorties into Kontum last night delivered 147 skids of 105mm how he (3758 rounds); 26 skids of 105mm illum, (628 rounds); and 29 skids of fuses (16,700). While additional sorties were scheduled, they were curtailed due to precautionary security measures which slowed down the operation. The JP-4 point at Kontum is being switched from a bladder to a blivit operation to allow for quick offload of JP-4 from the C-130.*

Although occasional closures of the runway resulted from the back-up of ammunition on the offload areas, 17 C-130 sorties resupplied Kontum City during the night of 24/25 May.[137/]

In other operations no significant progress was reported on the QL 14 "Rockpile" operation. A USAF FAC was killed while making a low level pass to resupply U.S. advisors at the Plei Mrong Ranger Camp. U.S. helicopters converged on the scene and recovered the body on the afternoon of the 24th.[138/]

All-Out Attack on Kontum City

Shortly after the last C-130 departed Kontum airfield on the night of 24/25 May, the USAF tower at the field reported that seven rounds of ordnance detonated on the southeastern edge of the runway. This was at 0510H, 25 May. By 0607H small enemy sapper units had penetrated to the

"Bishop's House," and to the eastern edge of the runway. Reports circulated that an enemy force of estimated reinforced company size had infiltrated and attacked the city from four directions, dressed in ARVN uniforms. 139/

At 0830H an enemy force led by tanks attacked the defensive line of the ARVN 53d Regiment from the north and northeast. U.S. and VNAF TACAIR responded and the initial thrust was repulsed. 140/ However, heavy incoming fire, primarily 122mm rockets and 105mm artillery, forced the closure of the runway. These ABFs hit the helicopter refueling point at the airport, and the 23d Division TOC. Brigadier General Hill, Senior Army Advisor to MR II, circled the besieged city in a helicopter and declared a TAC-E. This decision was based on several factors: intercepted enemy message traffic indicated reinforcements for the initial sapper force; aerial observations from his helicopter showed enemy troops moving in the area south of the city; and some three enemy battalions were either in or close to the southern and eastern edges of the city. Facing them were three friendly regiments in and around the city, and two battalions of the ARVN 44th Regiment, which attempted to return to Kontum City after engaging the enemy early that morning north of town. About 1545H, Gen Hill requested additional TACAIR to replace ARVN artillery neutralized by enemy shelling.

TACAIR now provided the only fire support for the ARVN infantry. The TACAIR provided was principally VNAF, as agreement had finally been reached with Gen Toan to cover the "Rockpile" with U.S. TACAIR and to use VNAF TACAIR in support of Kontum City. By 1730H all non-essential

U.S. personnel had been evacuated from Kontum City, and the airfield closed. The II DASC notified the 7th AF Tactical Air Control Center (TACC) that no C-130 resupply missions could safely land that night. As night fell, some enemy troops were lodged in Kontum City. [141/] In a related action to the south, Pleiku Air Base received 7x122mm rockets on the same day. Four VNAF helicopters were damaged, and several Montagnard refugees killed. Immediate action by VNAF Cobras resulted in the location and destruction of six of the eight enemy rocketeers. The area was quiet once again. [142/]

In spite of B-52 strikes and gunship sorties that night, at 0115H on the 26th enemy tanks and infantry attacked the 53d regiment again. Attacks on the eastern and southeastern perimeter coincided with this tank/infantry assault from the northeast. By 0300H the defensive line of the 53d had been breached, and by 0615H enemy tanks and troops moved to within 50 meters of the 44th Regiment Command Post. [143/]

One observer on the scene stated that the NVA must have had a "sorry weatherman," for just as the enemy attack rolled into high gear at dawn, the weather broke and allowed TACAIR and TOW-equipped UH-1 helicopters to engage the enemy armor. By 0856H the U.S. Air Cavalry had destroyed 10 tanks and a water tower held by the enemy with their TOW missiles.* One of these tanks had been previously damaged by a Spectre operating in the area. [144/]

*Five T-54s, two PT-76x, three disabled ARVN M-41s.

Refugees Flee Kontum City

FIGURE 7

U.S. TACAIR struck the ridge northwest of the city and silenced enemy artillery. An ARC LIGHT strike was planned for the same area that night, since intelligence reports indicated that the NVA 3d division from Binh Dinh might try to reinforce the 2d and 320th divisions in attacking Kontum City. Elements of the 2d NVA Division and the 28th Regiment had already engaged ARVN 23d Division units at the perimeter. As night fell, over 1,00 rounds of 105mm, 122mm and 155mm artillery and 122mm rockets had pounded the city, and the enemy elements remained lodged within it and along its perimeter. The TAC-E continued, and no C-130 resupply missions were flown into Kontum City. U.S. and VNAF CH-47 "Hooks," landing at the soccer field inside Kontum City, were the only source of resupply and medevac. Police and ARVN troops had to secure the area from swarms of refugees, who tried to force their way onto the helicopters leaving the besieged city.[145/] Just as VNAF and U.S. TACAIR sorties had covered Kontum City during the daylight hours of the 26th, so B-52 strikes and gunship coverage extended the protection of air into the night of the 26/27th. When a Spectre saw four tanks, one of which was firing at the city, he drove it off by engaging it with 40mm.

Although the ARVN 53d Regiment's defensive line in the northeast had been penetrated in several places, none of the panic evident at Tan Canh prevailed. While an ARVN battalion had run on the 26th, it quickly reformed and returned to its position. The tanks did not create the fear they had at Tan Canh, especially after the TOWs had eliminated many of them. On the morning of the 27th, ARVN soldiers armed with M-72 LAWs disposed of two more enemy tanks; the same toll was taken by TOW-equipped helicopters. The ARVN soldier began to get his feet on the ground; the enemy was no longer nine feet tall; the tanks were no longer invincible. When evacuation became necessary, as it did at FSB November on the 27th, it was orderly. [146/]

Weather remained unworkable for TACAIR on the morning of the 27th, although several sets of fighters were expended IFR in jettison boxes. A COMBAT SKY SPOT (CSS) attempt at 1130H failed due to radar difficulties, but by that time the weather cleared sufficiently for visual FAC targeting. The II Corps and 23d Division Commanders asked that CSS safe separation criteria be reduced from the 700 meter minimum to 500 meters, and they agreed to accept the responsibility for short rounds. Between 1600 and 0400H 27/28 May some 75 sorties of U.S. TACAIR served the Kontum City area; an average of better than one sortie every 10 minutes. [147/]

As the 27th drew to a close, the situation found the ARVN with the enemy lodged inside their perimeter, but they were unable to evict them. On the other hand, the NVA found themselves too weak to expand their perimeter and force their way into the inner city. A USAF advisor to the VNAF offered his opinion that [148/]

> the NVA itself helped save Kontum City by making numerous mistakes. First of all, they never made an all-out, coordinated effort where they used artillery, armor and infantry. Sometimes their infantry would get ahead of their tanks and vice-versa. On occasion they brought their tanks right down the open highway in single file.

There was no doubt that the enemy had made errors, and had been seriously hurt. Casualty figures for the period 14-27 May showed 2237 enemy KIA in the highlands versus friendly losses of 259.[149/]

The operation to reopen the Kontum pass continued to run hot and cold. ARVN Rangers had taken almost 20 percent casualties in the operation, but they tied down two NVA regiments that might have made the difference during the battle of Kontum City. TACAIR and B-52s continued to pound the "Rockpile," but the SRAG Chief of Staff noted that[150/]

> *in this pass clearing operation what we really have is an attack against a fortified position. This is not just an attack against hastily-dug fortifications; this is an attack of the magnitude of the attack against Casino in WW II. Some of the caves that the enemy is ensconced in have been noted to be as deep as 18 feet, making them impervious even to B-52 strikes. Because of this, and because ARVN has never had the preponderance of force which it could commit to this kind of operation and which it takes to be successful . . . we have a situation where neither adversary is strong enough . . . it's been a battle of attrition.*

Although the situation remained critical, ARVN forces began to counterattack and attempted to consolidate the perimeter. Efforts began on the 28th to disengage the enemy from the eastern end of the runway and the eastern portion of town. The southwestern portion had been secured, and a helicopter refueling point and a C-130 airdrop area were established there. The C-130 resupply by airdrop began that afternoon, and 50 of 64 bundles were recovered. The TAC-E remained in effect, and TACAIR punished the enemy moving on the ground. The arrival in Kontum City of an experienced

Covey FAC* and a radio operator promised better coordinated use of TACAIR at Kontum City. Several targets were struck with CBU 55s at the "Rockpile" and within Kontum City, while CSS targets were prepared in the event of poor weather.151/

The enemy had failed to route ARVN, or to achieve significant gains. They had made errors, such as the blowing of the Kontum City ammunition dump on the 27th preventing two of their own units from joining; and their whole attack was marked by lack of coordination.152/ By the 29th the senior USAF representative at II DASC reported that153/

> *although much of Kontum remains occupied by the enemy, principally the eastern and northern positions, Mr. Vann is greatly encouraged by the lack of enemy activity in and around the town last night and this morning. Mr. Vann told Lt Gen Toan that Quote: We may have turned this situation around. If so, it's only because of the absolutely tremendous ARC LIGHT and TACAIR support we've received in the past two nights. Unquote. Mr. Vann went on to say that we have prevented the enemy from moving and reinforcing during the times he normally could do so. Vann stated he could see no other reason why, with two enemy divisions confronting our forces, the enemy has failed to press the attack decisively. Mr. Vann also cautioned that we may be wrong and must keep up the pressure until the enemy withdraws.*

The situation was indeed "turned around" by air. During the 36-hour period from 271600H to 290400H, 203 U.S. TACAIR sorties were expended

*He had performed the same function at Quang Tri.

ARVN 23rd Division Gunners Defend the Perimeter

FIGURE 8

ARVN Soldiers Rost Out the Enemy in Kontum City

FIGURE 9

in MR II, principally in support of Kontum City. In addition, B-52 strikes and gunship flights kept the enemy constantly disoriented.[154/]

The enemy held basically the same positions on the 29th as he had the previous day. He occupied the east end of town from north to south, and many of the compounds across the north. The entire south side of the runway remained in enemy hands, and to the northwest a sizeable force occupied the low ground between the ARVN 45th Regiment and the northwest corner of town. Contacts remained close, but sporadic and light. A flanking movement by RF/PF troops caused the enemy to withdraw from the section of the west end of the runway. Resupply continued by C-130 airdrop, but only 24 of 48 bundles dropped that morning were immediately recovered. A recovery of the remainder was expected by ground personnel. Requests for more TACAIR were honored when ARVN planned a clearing action, but marginal weather at mid-morning limited such assistance both in Kontum City and the "Rockpile."[155/] Near the "Rockpile," at FSB 42, CBU-55 delivered on the 29th was reported "right on target" and "did an excellent job of destroying the enemy bunkers." Two more CBU sorties were scheduled for early morning of the 30th.[156/] Although the TAC-E continued on the 30th, the ground situation was relatively quiet in the city.* On the 31st, ARVN units continued to clear the enemy from the northern portions of the town, while RF units attacked and occupied enemy positions in southeastern Kontum City. Less than 100 rounds of

---

*President Nguyen Van Thieu visited the 23d Division TOC and promoted Col Ba, the Division Commander to Brigadier General on the 30th.

incoming artillery were reported, and at 0830H Mr. Vann terminated the TAC-E at Kontum City. The senior USAF representative recalled that Mr. Vann[157/]

> *expressed deep appreciation for the outstanding tactical air support provided to MR II during the emergency. Mr. Vann cautioned that in his view the lull in enemy activity may be only temporary, and requested air elements, specifically the Covey FACs, to conduct aggressive VR of their operational areas and rapidly report significant intelligence.*

To better use the Covey FACs (then stationed at DaNang), the senior USAF representative recommended that[158/]

> *some of our Coveys be positioned at Pleiku. I believe a minimum adequate posture would require two Coveys to RON each night . . . this procedure would virtually eliminate the possibility of workable morning weather and no FACs available to work.*

Weather problems between DaNang and Pleiku City prevented Covey FACs from arriving on station when planned or required. Beginning two days later one Covey FAC was to RON at Pleiku each night.

The Enemy Withdraws

By 1 June the enemy had ceased direct heavy pressure on Kontum City although three pockets of resistance remained in town. Fighting to expel or destroy these elements continued. Intelligence and VR indicated that the lull in activity might be short-lived, and SRAG expected resumption of the attack within four or five days. General Hill did not expect ARVN to aggressively expand the Kontum perimeter during the lull, citing ARVN's own weakened posture from the recent battle and disinclination for such operations. However, measures to harass and attrit the enemy were taken. General Hill ordered the Air Cavalry to undertake aggressive VR and ground team infiltration to the west and northwest. A Covey FAC would coordinate with the Air Cav and conduct airstrikes as required. The senior USAF representative at II DASC reported that 159/

> *Mr. Vann considers that our recent success in driving off the enemy at Kontum is due in large measure to the fact that we kept the enemy off-balance at night with gunships, ARC LIGHT, COMBAT SKY SPOT, LORAN releases, and visual strikes. He requests that the TACAIR fragged to MR II during the past two nights be increased to continue the pressure on the enemy.*

Clearing operations continued on 2 June at the southern and eastern end of the runway, and at the two northern pockets of resistance. The C-130 drop zone was moved to the northwest corner of town, inside defensive positions held by the ARVN 45th Regiment. Sporadic shelling continued throughout the day. Although the fighting was slowing down, losses were almost inevitable. For example at 1100H a U.S. "Huey" helicopter was shot down near FSB 41 while enroute from Pleiku to Kontum. The Army pilot was killed and two officers severely injured. One of the two was the USAF Air Liaison Officer (ALO) advisor to the ARVN 23d Division. During the critical days at Kontum City he had functioned single-handedly as both VNAF ALO advisor, and U.S. Tactical Air Control Party (TACP). Tragedy continued to follow the operation when the first pilot of an Army rescue helicopter was killed by small arms fire. A third Army helicopter rescued the survivors, but the USAF ALO died enroute to a hospital outside the war zone.[160/] In the Chu Pao pass, two additional ranger battalions were committed to the clearing operation, and began moving from the Plei Mrong Ranger Camp to the west end of the "Rockpile." The camp, and nearby FSB 41, received light ABFs during the day. On the east coast of MR II, in Binh Dinh province, attacks were expected at LZ Crystal following a heavy ABF. Gunships, Tum FACs and CSS targets were assigned to the area.[161/]

The runway remained closed on the 3rd, but reduction of enemy pockets surrounding it continued. The north (hospital) compound was further reduced, and other engagements took place outside the northwestern perimeter. It appeared that several major NVA units were pulling back from Kontum City to the area north and east of town. A POW claimed over 2100 replacements had been sent to NVA units during May to take part in the highlands battles. Air and ARVN had taken their toll, and a Ranger battalion sweeping west of the "Rockpile" reported finding another 100 enemy KBA.[162/]

Major action shifted to the LZ Crystal/Phu My area on the east coast. The senior U.S. advisor at LZ Crystal declared a TAC-E, but this was cancelled by General Hill. The policy was announced that only Mr. Vann or he would declare a TAC-E in MR II. Since poor weather in the highlands precluded visual work in the area, most of the TACAIR was sent to LZ Crystal. When the senior USAF representative at II DASC phoned the LZ

to ask about the air support, they answered with an "enthusiastic" yes.
They were very pleased with the TACAIR support. Some 40 enemy were reported
KBA after the brief engagement. Tum FACs worked the area, but were not
manned for 24-hour operation, and 7AF was requested to task the 21st
Tactical Air Support Squadron (TASS) for augmentees.[163/]

Air drop C-130 resupply continued on the 4th, as the runway remained
closed. ARVN units cleared the southeastern corner of Kontum City and the
45th regiment continued sweeping the northwestern section of the city meeting
very little resistance. The mopping-up operations called for little TACAIR,
and only four CSS sorties flew in the Kontum area during the period 040400H
and 041600H. In contrast, 60 sorties flew to the threatened LZ Crystal/
Phu My area on the east coast.[164/]

High winds and rain continued to lash the highlands into the 5th,
making air operations unfeasible except on the east coast. Clearing
operations continued in Kontum City, and the runway was secured. ARVN
engineers began repairing damage to the runway, but the Ground-Controlled
Approach (GCA) unit and runway lights were still out. Aerial resupply
therefore continued using MSQ-directed parachute drops. Kontum City continued to receive occasional incoming, as did Pleiku AB and LZ Crystal.
An ARVN relief column had reached the latter, and the enemy's hopes of an
easy victory vanished.[165/] As the enemy's strength seemed to wane, ARVN's
aggressiveness increased. An intelligence bulletin of 6 June stated that[166/]

> *General Toan, MR II Commander, has offered 50,000
> Piaster rewards to his men for the destruction or
> capture of NVA tanks. This financial incentive
> has resulted in spirited competition and increased
> aggressiveness on the part of many friendly
> soldiers in the face of enemy tanks.*

Action at SRAG and II Corps HQ intensified on the 6th, when intelligence reports from monitored enemy transmissions indicated that another all-out tank/infantry attack against Kontum City would begin late that afternoon. In preparation II DASC requested the following air support: 167/

    1. Increased TACAIR, including CSS, to begin at 1930H at 30 minute intervals, instead of the fragged 1.5-2.0 hour intervals.

    2. Stationing of a PAVE AEGIS (105mm equipped) gunship.

    3. Maximum flare capability for all gunships assigned.

    4. A second Covey FAC to RON at Pleiku AB that night.

    5. SRAG, in concert with ARVN, to develop divert targets for the B-52s near possible enemy assembly points.

    6. A PAVE NAIL FAC and F-4s with laser-guided bombs to strike four bridges vital to the enemy's logistics.

Air drops, helicopter resupply and evacuation of wounded continued throughout the day, as ARVN began to clear the one remaining enemy pocket in the northeastern portion of the city. Government troops found many enemy bodies and weapons left behind by the retreating foe. Operations near the "Rockpile" began to move as well, and Task Force 21 had proceeded 6 km that morning and were now 15 km northeast of Plei Mrong.

In response to a request from 7AF concerning LORAN aircraft provided to MR II since 25 May, II DASC responded that[168/]

> *the only day since 25 May that DASC records indicate receiving substantial LORAN aircraft assistance is 31 May (15 aircraft). We do not normally make LORAN releases when FACs are working VFR. On the other hand, during peak ARC LIGHT periods it is difficult to obtain SKY SPOT MSQ service, and LORAN aircraft are very helpful in bad weather. This morning I requested Deputy Director, II DASC to prepare a message to 7AF requesting 2 LORAN Pathfinder aircraft daily during the rainy season in Pleiku.*

The expected enemy attack failed to materialize, and work began on the 7th to put the runway back into operation. Half of an Army GCA unit was already in position, with the other half due in by airlift that afternoon. Air drop and helicopter resupply continued in the interim. Weather wavered between unworkable and marginal causing two sorties with LGBs to return to base (RTB). Seventeen of the Kontum TACAIR sorites during 070400H and 071600H were LORAN releases, and II DASC noted that "the increased availability of Pathfinder aircraft made MR II TACAIR operations much more flexible, less dependent on the MSQ schedule during bad weather, and reduced the necessity to use TACAN releases as a last resort."[169/]

ARVN II Corps reported the following results of enemy and friendly losses during the battle for Kontum 14 May-6 June:[170/]

    1. Friendly Losses: 382 KIA, 1621 WIA, 32 MIA. Four crew served weapons destroyed, 47 small arms lost, 6 radios lost, 3 tanks 100% destroyed, 4 tanks 30% damaged.

2. Enemy losses: 5688 KIA, 34 POW, 8* Hoi Chanh, 353 crew-served weapons captured, 862 small arms captured, 29 radios captured, 38 tanks destroyed.

The II DASC stated that 171/

> *many of the enemy casualties were inflicted by USAF and VNAF TACAIR. Enemy tanks destoyed are believed to include some abandoned ARVN tanks that had been captured by the enemy (and those destroyed at Tan Canh also). I estimate that a very large number of enemy KBA at Kontum are not included in the above, since the target areas of most ARC LIGHT and TACAIR sorties in direct support of Kontum have not been swept by friendly forces. At 0908H today the one thousandth ARC LIGHT strike in MR II since 1 Jan 72 occurred. The occasion was marked by a small ceremony in II Corps G-2 at which toasts were drunk to USAF and SAC.*

Early on the 8th, ARVN continued to eliminate the last pocket of enemy resistance at 1-1/2 km north of the runway. The runway itself was now open, and the GCA reported as operational although not yet checked by USAF flight check aircraft. No incoming was reported, and friendly troops sweeping the area continued to find enemy bodies in abandoned bunkers. Air drop sorties continued and "II Corps G-4 reports that air drops, using MSG, have been very accurate, and nearly all parachute bundles are impacting in the recovery area." 172/ Slow ground recovery presented a problem, but the II Corps Commander directed additional manpower be provided for the task.

By midmorning II DASC announced that "the reported pocket of enemy resistance 1-1/2 km north of the runway has been eliminated. There is no

---

*Could not make out in source document whether the figure for the "Open Arms" ralliers was eight or 88.

organized enemy resistance reported in town.[173/] Mr. Vann considered runway resupply urgent, and requested resumption that night. II DASC agreed that C-130 night operations into Kontum now presented the same level of risk as they had prior to the attack on the city. The danger from enemy rocket and artillery fire still existed, but each C-130 was instructed to contact Carbon Outlaw (II DASC) for final clearance before beginning its GCA blackout approach to the airfield. The same procedure was in effect after takeoff, prior to clearing the next aircraft. If the 23d Division TOC reported enemy activity in town or near the airfield to II DASC, the aircraft were not permitted to land. By 0600H on the 9th, six C-130s had delivered cargo to Kontum City. Daylight aerial drops continued as well.[174/]

The Death of John Paul Vann

Disaster struck at the hour when victory was near at hand. At 2115H 9 June, Mr. John Paul Vann, Senior U.S. Advisor to MR II, departed Pleiku City in his light observation helicopter (LOH) to spend the night in Kontum City. His pilot and another Army officer accompanied him. At about 2130H ARVN soldiers at FSBs 41 and 41a, near the "Rockpile" reported seeing a helicopter on fire. They further saw it crash and continue burning. II DASC was notified at 2145H and sent Covey 46 to assist in the rescue operations. He arrived on scene at 2155H, and was joined by two Army helicopters and Spectre 18 by 2215H. Nail 76 replaced Covey 46 at 2225H and directed the on-scene search using an Army helicopter and Spectre's air and ground burning flares, infra-red (IR), and illuminator. They located the wreckage at 2300H at coordinates ZA 205704, a short distance east of highway QL 14. ARVN ground troops from FSB 41a moved to the crash site and reported all three dead. At about 2330H Bambino 39, the Army helicopter, landed at the site and identified one of the bodies as that of Mr. Vann. Nail 76 and Spectre 18 had shown outstanding teamwork and professionalism in their efforts, and General Hill commended the Air Force for its outstanding support--but the flamboyant, the skilled, the incomparable John Paul Vann was dead. An era had ended. 175/

On 10 June General Hill was replaced on normal rotation by Colonel (Brigadier General Selectee) Kingston, USA. Brigadier General Healy, USA, arrived to replace Mr. Vann. The two senior advisory positions in MR II had changed in less than 24 hours. 176/

CHAPTER IV

USAF AND VNAF AIR IN THE DEFENSE OF THE CENTRAL HIGHLANDS

This brief chapter is generally devoted to the personal recollections and opinions of U.S. advisors, primarily those on the ground, who were directly affected by the role air played in the defense of the Central Highlands. This is not a cold statistical approach,* but an attempt to provide the honest impressions of those who lived the battles.

There are many references throughout the first three chapters of this report to the role B-52s, gunships, and TACAIR played, and these will be recapitulated only briefly. Problem areas, when documented, will also be mentioned.

The Role of the B-52s

The huge strategic bombers were used primarily in a tactical role. by dropping their ordnance into pre-planned boxes, or delivering it as close as 1000 meters in front of friendly defensive lines, the B-52s became the air weapon the enemy feared most. Whether used in an anti-logistics or in an anti-personnel/close - fire support role they became the silent terror. As one advisor put it: 177/

> *It's a known fact that the greatest thing the enemy fears is the B-52s. They can see a Covey FAC or an*

---

*The tables and charts in the appendix to this report provide some statistical data. An excellent source of such data is the Monthly HQ PACAF Summary of Air Operations in South East Asia.

> *O-1 flying over, but they never know when those B-52 bombs are going to come raining down on them...I'm convinced it was the B-52s that saved Kontum the way they were employed.*

The senior U.S. advisor to the ARVN 23d Division in Kontum City recalled [178/] that

> *Once penetrations were made and they pulled the plug on B-52 strikes, we employed them much in the same manner as our close defensive artillery. As a matter of fact, this is one of the functions they performed, and they do the job much better than artillery. It was extremely important because the only ammo supply we had was in our positions. We had lost our ammo dump and our resupply had been cut down to nothing. I think that airpower played an extremely vital role, allowing us to conserve artillery ammunition for when we had to use artillery. With the application of the B-52 strikes I feel they really saved the day, because after them the NVA was never able to come in again and significantly reinforce or resupply the lodgements they had made in the city. We estimate about 3 regiments were within the defense perimeter. In essence, airpower - tactical air and the B-52's - served as a shield which allowed us to pull enough infantry strength off the perimeter line to come back into the interior of the position and eliminate the lodgements that had been made.*

A USAF Covey FAC who worked the Kontum City area during the battle [179/] recalled:

> "*There's no doubt in my mind that if it weren't for the B-52s and other air that Kontum would have fallen. The ARVN would sit in their bunkers and call for more and more air, closer and closer. I bombed two days inside the city. I found out later that's what helped destroy the 3 regiments which got into the city.*"

Finally, the comments of Brigadier General Ba, the Commander of the ARVN 23d Division: [180/]

> *I must say that the air gave us (a) very good
> support. Support like I have never seen before...
> If the B-52s strike only strategic targets they
> can strike only Hanoi. From the 17th parallel
> south I say that the best strategic targets for
> the B-52s is right in front of my positions.
> That means from 5 klicks to 2 klicks (km), because
> that's where the VC regroup before they attack
> the positions. I think that's a strategic target
> where the VC group for an assault...We must use the
> B-52 in close support to the front lines.*

General Creighton Abrams, COMUSMACV, sent a message of congratulations to 8AF in Guam. He said that[181/]

> *as the current offensive campaign extends into its
> seventh week, I am increasingly impressed with the
> contribution that the ARC LIGHT program has made.
> There is no question that the B-52s have been a
> major factor, and on occasion the deciding factor,
> in preventing the enemy's accomplishment of most
> of his major goals.*

The Role of U.S. TACAIR

The rapid deployment of the United States Navy and United States Marine Corps air arms, in addition to a large augmentation of the USAF forces, created a veritable air armada to combat the enemy invasion. While initial problems arose in orienting newly assigned "fast mover" pilots to the area and to their mission, they soon became skilled at their wartime tasks. There was no disputing the inherent advantages of the F-4s, A-7s, and A-4s: ability to respond to an emergency and get to the target area quickly, greater survival rate against all but the most sophisticated* enemy anti-aircraft weapon, and great accuracy when using the new laser-guided bombs. There were, however, inherent disadvantages as well: short time on target (TOT) when laden with ordnance, restricted use in poor weather unless using sophisticated electronic methods, usually in conjuction with ground stations, and questionable accuracy at times when using freefall bombs. On the latter point, the senior USAF representatives at II DASC commented on "fast mover saturation bombing":[182/]

> *"The accuracy of bombing thus far by the mission aircraft has been totally unacceptable. On one instance approximately 96 MK-82's were placed on a bridge that should have been destroyed by 2. Results of the 96 bombs - one bridge slightly damaged."*

Other problem areas appeared with ordnance changes on the frag aircraft. A Covey FAC flying the Kontum area noted that[183/]

> *the problem all the FACs have is getting a fast enough change of ordnance. For the first part of the offensive we couldn't get any snake or napalm, all we could get were slick bombs for high-angle dive bombing. You can't do close air support with fast moving aircraft. It's difficult-they don't have enough holding time and they can't make several passes because they don't have enough fuel. The F-4 is just not a good close air support aircraft... When they were making these attacks out in the open, we couldn't get nape, CBU or Rockeye. All we could get was slick hard bombs. Any of our fast moving aircraft going below a 3000 feet deck and trying to bomb a moving tank is trying to shoot a fish in a lake with a .22 off the bank.*

However, there was no question but that the "fast mover" TACAIR

---

*No SAM launchings were reported in MR II.

saved many of the FSB's from being overrun, effectively destroyed war material abandoned by ARVN or massed by the enemy, and provided a shield for friendly forces when used in a troop or logistics interdiction role.

The Role of The U.S. Gunships*

The enemy broke off many engagements merely by the appearance of a gunship on the scene. The AC-119 Stingers and AC-130 Spectres often provided the only available air during crucial contacts. For example, on the morning of 25 May the initial enemy forces attacking Kontum City were held off by VNAF TACAIR and Spectres. The effectiveness of the 20 and 40mm guns on the Spectres and the addition of the 105mm "big gun" on the PAVE AEGIS (C-130-E) Spectres made the AC-130s a much respected and feared weapon system.

The added electronic sophistication of the AC-130, in comparison to the AC-119, made it a more versatile gunship system. Among the roles the AC-130 performed were armed reconnaissance, tank and truck killer, general interdiction of troops and supplies, close air support under TIC conditions, the use of the 2kw light to mark targets and drop zones for other aircraft, artillery suppression and destruction, dropping of flares to aid FACs or ground troops, escort aircraft and AAA suppression for C-130 cargo planes, acting as a FAC for TACAIR, and search and rescue (SAR) support.

Among the innovative tactics developed by the Spectres was that

*Information for this section came primarily from a draft copy of the 16th SOS Quarterly History, March-June 1972.

of firing off the inertial navigation system (INS) in a TIC environment.
This all-weather tactic was introduced by Spectre 03 near Dak Pek on
10 June. The weather was bad with 7/8 cloud cover, and the ground
commander did not have an X-band beacon. As the situation on the
ground became more critical, the crew of Spectre 03 manually fed in
coordinates to the gunship's fire control and INS computers. Since
the gunship's LORAN was inoperative at the time, initial coordinates
were determined by dropping flares near suspected friendly positions
and receiving ground verification of these. The navigator tracked
this position by sensor and updated his computer to the known reference.
With this knowledge, target coordinates provided by the ground commander
were fed into the computer. An initial trial run was then made on this
position to make certain that it did not threaten friendly troops.
Using corrections given by the ground commander, the crew was able to
continually adjust their fire to successful strike enemy targets.
Spectre 03 expended 62 rounds of 105mm and 216 of 40mm in this fashion.
At no time did the gunship fire less that 500 meters from friendly
positions. The enemy ABF and ground action ceased, and some 50 of them
were reported KBA.

    The gunships initially experienced some problems with FACs and II
DASC personnel who did not fully understand the AC-119s and AC-130s
versatility and capability. This was hardly surprising, since the
gunships primary AO had been in Laos and Cambodia prior to the 1972
offensive in South Vietnam. Spectre 19 reported on 2 May that 184/

> Covey 564 calls Carbon Outlaw requesting a gunship to work suspected TIC...almost unbelievably Carbon Outlaw says he has no gunship available. We call and tell him that Spectre 19 is a gunship. He says, "Stand By"....These people in MR II have no foggy idea of how to make use of an AC-130. Carbon Outlaw simply ran us from one FAC to another, hoping that one of them would not be working higher priority TACAIR. (At one point we had word from 7AF that we had priority over fighters; this is most definitely not the case). Until such time as Carbon Outlaw figures out how to make effective use of Spectre, I strongly recommend no further daytime sorties to MR II. In fact, why are we flying these day frags at all when we get kicked off almost every target by "high priority" fighter strikes?

Having to make way for the fighters was perhaps "sour grapes," but a far more serious problem was reported by Spectre 15 on 6 May: [185/]

> At 2310 a COMBAT SKY SPOT was released over Tango's position. There were no guard warnings, and Carbon Outlaw and Rocket 44 were both unaware that the strike was to be held. The bombs fell through our altitudes on all sides narrowly missing us. Tango wasn't so lucky - 5 bombs impacted inside his compound wounding 15 persons...

A Covey FAC reported a similar occurrence. He stated that B-52 strikes [186/]

> almost knocked me down three times in two days. working down in the valleys like we are, you don't get all the DART transmissions. B-52s just can't come up on Guard, I don't know what the problem is that they can't broadcast from that high an altitude to the valley. They walked right across my tail less than 1/4 mile. I sure have a lot of respect for the B-52s, and I think they're doing a tremendous job; but there sure ought to be a better safety program.

Often Stingers, Spectres and TACAIR were fragged to the same targets, but this did not present the same problems as did unannounced Army or

VNAF aircraft. Spectre 19 reported on 9 May:[187/]

> 0425. For the second time a "Spooky" (VNAF C-47) gunship pulled into the area we were trying to work. Communication with these people is impossible, and if some form of controlling them isn't developed; we're going to have some friendly BDA one of these nights.

These problem areas were noted by 7AF, and in a message to the 8th Tactical Fighter Wing (TFW) at Ubon, improvements were promised in some of these matters. The availability and use of the X-band beacons would be stressed with the U.S. Army, and all FACs and DASC personnel had been briefed several times on gunship operations and capabilities.[188/] Indeed, as the offensive continued, the gunship became the second most-feared air weapon after the B-52s; and because of its versatility it became a mainstay in the defense of the Central Highlands.

Other Air Resources

Not enough can be said about the C-130 crews, who risked their lives and aircraft so Kontum City would survive. During the 40 days between 22 May and 30 June, they made some 95 air drops and 284 landings in MR II, primarily at Kontum and Pleiku cities.[189/] They provided ARVN with the rations and material needed to press the fight to a favorable conclusion. Totally dependent upon other aircraft or ground forces for protection, the crews of these lumbering giants braved AAA, artillery rounds, rockets and small arms fire to deliver the vital goods. It is no wonder that many of their fellow pilots say that the C-130 crews have the most guts in South East Asia.

The U.S. Air Cavalry, with its supply, medevac and gunship helicopters, certainly performed many vital functions. The introduction of the helicopter-mounted TOW missile brought a new, lethal anti-tank weapon to the highlands at a critical phase.

In effect, all types of aircraft were mobilized to defeat the enemy invasion. From the small O-2 FAC aircraft, to the giant B-52s, all played their roles in preventing defeat.

Problems With BDA/KBA

The senior USAF representatives at II DASC pointed out problems with vehicle BDA on 10 May. He reported that 190/

> *accounting for vehicles destroyed during combat conditions involving ground troops with vehicle killer weapons, TAC-AIR, U.S. Army Air Cav and possibly other forces sometimes becomes a problem. In some cases, more than one force claims the same kill when both are engaging the same target. Another problem is the ability of the enemy to immediately tow away or camouflage a vehicle that has just been struck.*
>
> *During the Tan Canh tank attack a relatively accurate tank destruction account was maintained. Each day after this battle a number of tanks and trucks previously counted as destroyed began to disappear. . . . They were either moved, camouflaged or buried, etc., . . . The enemy has been reported to have dozens of troops following each vehicle with tree branches erasing its tracks. When the vehicle stops, these troops put their tree branches over the vehicles to hide them. . . .*
>
> *When I monitor an air strike or attack on radio I attempt to keep an account of the results. . . . An accountability problem again arose in the attack on Ben Het . . . TACAIR, Spectre gunships, U.S. Army Cobra gunships and ground friendly force M-72 teams all*

> *attacked these vehicles within a short period of time.
> . . . All three were destroyed . . . these vehicles could
> easily have been counted as six destroyed. . . . I will
> always have good reasons for any BDA claims, and I lean
> toward the conservative.*

The accounting of KBA figures proved even more difficult. On the one hand, it was next to impossible to get ARVN to patrol beyond the perimeter. On the other hand, when ARVN did go out and report BDA/KBA they often "turned one NVA body over four ways."[191/] While this may have been true in certain cases, John Paul Vann said that[192/]

> *it should be noted that the ARVN have consistently
> refrained from reporting either TACAIR or B-52 KBA
> results that have not been confirmed by ground sweep.
> For that reason, it is my opinion that reported enemy
> casualties reflect only a small percentage of the
> actual damage the enemy has suffered.*

By the time many of the ARVN ground sweeps took place, the enemy had buried or carried off its dead. As previously stated in the report, estimates of enemy KBA ran to 40 percent of the entire attacking force in the Central Highlands.

The SA-7 Threat

The Soviet-made SA-7* was a low altitude, surface-to-air, heat-seeking missile which could be hand carried and fired. Much like the U.S. "Redeye," the SA-7 had an operating range of two to three nautical miles and could reach altitudes of 10,000-12,000 feet. It was capable of downing aircraft traveling up to 430 knots.[193/]

*Soviet designation "Strella" or "Strela." NATO designation "Grail."

Although the SA-7 had been reported and confirmed in MRs I and III, the first possible sighting of an SA-7 in MR II occurred on 10 June. Two Army U-21 pilots and a passenger observed a missile apparently tracking an F-4 on his pullout from a dive bombing attack near Kontum City. The observers reported they were at 9500 feet MSL, and that the missile burnout was at an estimated 7000 feet MSL. One of the U-21 pilots had seen an A-1 shot down near An Loc by an SA-7 and he believed that he had witnessed another SA-7. The introduction of the missile into MR II had been expected because of its confirmed effectiveness in other areas. The only question which bothered the senior USAF representative at II DASC was why the enemy had chosen to disclose the SA-7 capability against an F-4, rather than a C-130 or other slow mover. He recommended though, that night runway resupply be discontinued until conditions were more secure. The SRAG staff considered the recommendation "premature," and stressed the need for aerial resupply as long as QL 14 remained closed.[194/] The decision was made to continue night runway resupply in spite of dangers involved to the cargo aircraft.

The Senior Air Force Representative was tasked by 7AF to devise procedures to minimize the SA-7 threat to the C-130s during their most vulnerable period, i.e., just prior to landing at Kontum. A three phase plan was developed to accomplish this task. First, friendly forces were ordered to occupy the area from which the SA-7 was reported launched - approximately four kilometers due east of the east end of the runway on high ground. Next the Senior Air Force Representative arranged a coordinated fire support plan. As C-130s reported on downwind, GCA had an artillery liaison officer who ordered suppressive artillery fire on the flanks of the friendly forces noted above. Finally as the aircraft turned base leg, an artillery flare shell was fired in the vicinity of the final approach in the hope that it would attract any SA-7 fired at the aircraft. These procedures were in effect for six days at which time the enemy was pushed from Kontum, significantly decreasing the threat to the landing aircraft.

The crew of Spectre 07 reported possible SA-7 launches on 10 and 11 June. They launched an XLUU flare on both occasions as a diversion and the missile did not strike the aircraft.[195/] There was also a report of a possible SA-7 launch against a C-130 about to land at Kontum City airfield on 13 June. However, no corroborating evidence was obtained, and it was speculated that a flare dropped by a Covey FAC near the GCA base leg might have been mistaken for a missile.[196/]

Although no aircraft had been downed in MR II by an SA-7 during the period of this report a potent antiaircraft weapon had made its appearance.

VNAF Performance

USAF could justifiably be proud of VNAF performance in MR II. The small force which had been trained, equipped and nurtured by USAF had now become the sixth largest air force in the world. Where ARVN generally suffered from lack of leadership and fighting spirit, VNAF had a surfeit of esprit'-de-corps among its elite pilot force. It was not uncommon for VNAF A-1 or A-37 pilots to have 4,000 or more flying hours in their aircraft, or for them to fly four or more missions per day. VNAF was a subordinate arm of ARVN, and not a separate and equal service. This relationship often presented problems of communication and coordination, but when given a mission VNAF pilots performed magnificently. A USAF advisor to VNAF recalled that[197/]

> *John Paul Vann came in just elated at the VNAF performance. They were getting right down on the deck and putting their butt right on the line. There was murderous fire there, because the NVA had brought down numerous 51 cal quad 50's; they had even 23mm AAA guns up there and those guys were going right down the barrel . . . John Paul Vann came in so excited and said: That's the best damn bombing I've seen in my 11 years over here! That was his estimation of the VNAF. I don't think you need any more testimony than that. In the defense of Kontum the VNAF has been magnificent, absolutely magnificent.*

Within its limited resources, VNAF did an outstanding job. VNAF fixed-wing cargo planes could not resupply Kontum City at night because their crews were not night-qualified, but VNAF CH-47 and "Slick" helicopters resupplied the city and the FSBs during some of the heaviest fighting. The VNAF helicopter gunships took four times as many hits as any other VNAF aircraft. VNAF medevac helicopters went into Kontum City during the daylight hours, and during some of the heaviest action.[198/]

VNAF came into its own during the 1972 offensive, and supported the campaign in the highlands to the maximum of its capability.

Air Power and the Battle for Kontum

There was no disagreement from any source when air power, specifically the U.S. air armada, was given credit for preventing a South Vietnamese defeat during the current offensive. The senior U.S. advisor to the ARVN 23d Division stated that [199/]

> *the Vietnamese here were probably better supported by airpower than in any other engagements I've seen including the 1968 Tet offensive. I think this assisted in giving them the confidence that they needed to stay and make a fight of it.*

A USAF advisor to VNAF echoed these sentiments when he said that [200/]

> *what we have done with the use of U.S. air is to allow the South Vietnamese to maintain their country while they continue to become strong. That to me has been the role of U.S. air at Kontum. We've allowed the South Vietnamese to fight very capably at Kontum.*

In conclusion, there was probably no better summation of the role air power played in the defense of Kontum City than that spoken by the HQ SRAG Chief of Staff. He said that [201/]

> *undoubtedly, airpower played a critically important role. As one looks back, one could say there were many ifs on the battlefield. For example, one would make the case that if it had not been for John Paul Vann, the battle could have been lost. One could make the case that if it had not been for the presence of Gen. Hill over Kontum on the 26th of May that the battle could have been lost. If it had not been for the TOWs at a critical point in time, the battle could have been lost. Many of these "ifs" are possible. However, one "if" is a certainty--that if it had not been for U.S. airpower the battle would have been lost.*

CHAPTER V

CONCLUSION

A New ARVN Aggressiveness

A U.S. intelligence source stated that [202/]

> at the start of the VC/NVA offensive, which is on a larger scale than any ever before mounted by the North Vietnamese (and which has effectively scotched the fiction Hanoi has been trying to maintain that the fighting is an indigenous "rebellion") South Vietnamese forces had never faced a conventional attack of such magnitude. It was moreover the first time ARVN had been called on to fight in major actions without the presence of U.S. ground forces in South Vietnam. The lack of confidence (and experience) on the part of both ARVN troops and their commanders was reflected in the events which marked the first part of the enemy offensive, the loss of Quang Tri City under questionable circumstances, the defeat at Tan Canh in the western highlands, and the overrunning of Loc Ninh in Binh Long Province. ARVN did not collapse under these physical and psychological blows, however, and instead dug in along new defensive lines where they have hung on tenaciously. Thanks in part to heavy U.S. air support, VN/NVA thrusts in MR-II have been contained and repelled, the attack on Kontum City was so decisively defeated that the two VC/NVA divisions involved have pulled back to lick their wounds, and the city of An Loc has held.

A U.S. advisor to the ARVN 23d Division commented that defensively [203/]

> the ARVN here at Kontum did very well; offensively, by our own standards, they don't move as aggressively, but this is the first time this division has worked together. We're building a new division right now; one that had never been up against the NVA before. . . . Collectively I'm very proud of the ARVN performance during this battle.

Allegations were made that the ARVN 23d Division did not run from Kontum City as the 22d had at Tan Canh because there was no place to run to. QL 14 between Kontum and Pleiku cities was cut, and VC/NVA units held the vital pass. The Chief of Staff, HQ SRAG commented on this and said[204/]

> *that has been alleged, of course. Undoubtedly it did play a psychological role with the ARVN. However, remember that you don't need to have an open road for units to disappear: to put on civilian clothes, and evaporate. These things did not happen in any great magnitude during the battle of Kontum. It cannot be stated that the closure of the pass was the reason that the ARVN stayed and fought. They could have stayed and have given up, for example, but they stayed and they fought.*

One of the American advisors admitted that when left to their own devices, ARVN and VNAF could usually do the job, even if they floundered initially; but he added that[205/]

> *we're Americans, and a very impatient group of people. When this battle was joined, we were in fact directing the air power. We would influence the action by our communication with higher headquarters. We were thinking rationally in many cases where the Vietnamese became very excited. What are you going to do? When your damn butt's on the line, what are you going to do. Are you going to sit back and say I've failed, I'm not a successful advisor because I can't get my counterparts to do what he's supposed to do - or take over . . . When your neck's out on the line you're going to do as you've been trained and take over.*

Leadership, always a weak point in the ARVN structure, took a positive turn with the appointment of General Toan as II Corps Commander and

Brigadier General Ba as Commander of the 23d ARVN Division at Kontum City. Both were aggressive individuals, and a U.S. advisor said General Ba has 206/

> *his complete unit there, he knows his commanders and he's doing a hell of a good job. He's on the offensive right now to regain territory and build confidence in his unit, and go out and find the enemy.*

The 23d Division indeed became more aggressive, and by the latter part of June it patrolled some 9 km, beyond its perimeter. On 17 June a successful ARVN/VNAF planned and executed operation took place at Tan Canh, and many refugees were helilifted out of the area. By 29 June a 30-vehicle Military Convoy passed through the "Rockpile," reopening QL 14 from Pleiku to Kontum cities. On the east coast, after initial reverses at Phu My, ARVN offensive operations brought the Binh Dinh Province towns captured by the enemy in early April under government control. By 29 July all three district towns were in ARVN hands.

Airpower, while providing ARVN with tremendous support, could not be the total answer. Airpower, in and of itself, cannot insure victory; but in combination with a spirited ground defense it can prevent defeat. As the Chief of Staff, HQ SRAG put it: 207/

> *One of the "ifs" we can refer to, is if the ARVN hadn't had the fortitude and the guts to stay in Kontum no amount of airpower could have prevented the loss of Kontum. So, we can say that ARVN in that case performed magnificently.*

Enemy Reactions and Future Plans

Late in July an article in the Los Angeles Times stated that [208/]

> American officials speculate that the supply problem prompted Hanoi to abandon its offensive in the Highlands. Within the last few weeks evidence has mounted that Hanoi has literally written off this campaign.
>
> Intelligence readouts indicate that the Viet Cong 2d Division* has moved back into sanctuary areas from its positions north of Kontum and that the regiments of the 320th Division, which were to capture the city, have pulled back in Laos. South Vietnamese intelligence sources claim the commanders of both were recalled and reprimanded by Lt Gen Hoang Minh Thao, the overall commander, who led a division at Dien Bien Phu.
>
> At any rate, Kontum is now being regularly supplied by truck convoys and the shelling of the city has all but ceased - an indication that the 40th North Vietnamese Artillery Regiment has also been pulled back into Laos as military intelligence officers claim.

A 90-day intelligence assessment of enemy gains and losses throughout SVN during the offensive concluded that: [209/]

> - the enemy still held most of the limited gains achieved in the first month of the fighting, but increased ARVN aggressiveness was reversing this stand.
>
> - the enemy had failed to fatally damage ARVN, which was now stronger numerically and more effective in combat than at the start of the enemy offensive

*This should be NVA 2d Division.

> - the momentum of the enemy drive was largely gone, and his thrust in the western highlands had been defeated with heavy casualties.
>
> - the enemy had paid a heavy price in men and materials for what they achieved. The enemy may have lost as many as 40,000 killed, and 450 tanks.
>
> - expended enemy supplies will be difficult, if not impossible to replace because of the damage done by renewed U.S. bombing of North Vietnam and the closure of the North Vietnamese ports.*
>
> - the South Vietnamese population showed little popular support for the VC/NVA cause during the offensive.
>
> - enemy forces remain formidable despite their losses and probably have the capability to obtain some replacements and supplies. New attacks might be mounted, although not on the earlier scale. Hanoi might try to achieve more substantial gains before bargaining at the peace talks.

What had happened to the enemy in the Central Highlands? He had been beaten, and had withdrawn to lick his wounds. A Covey FAC flying the area noted that[210/]

> all the traffic we've seen since 10 June has been moving west. All the trucks we find are going into Laos; all the troops are going west into Laos.

Did this mean the enemy had been permanently drive out of the Central Highlands, or was he merely refitting to return at the beginning of the dry season? The only predictability concerning VC/NVA aims and future plans remained their unpredictability but for the time being RVN had successfully thwarted a North Vietnamese takeover of the area.

*A USAF advisor to the VNAF said that ARVN forces captured an enemy tank intact at Kontum City because it had run out of gas.

MR II FLOWN SORTIES MAR - APR 1972

	29	30	31	1	2	3	4	5	6	7	8	9	10	11	12	13	14	15	16	17	18	19
VNAF	25	44	40	40	64	58	34	37	35	45	26	42	49	44	46	52	60	42	32	46	40	44
USMC													8	17	11	4	22	14	18	18	18	18
USN	4	2	6																			
ARC LIGHT	27	24	21	15	2	15	7	82	12	29	71	57	65	30	34	53	32	44	14	97	42	22
GUNSHIPS							21	12	20	21	13	9	27	28	15	21	27	14	18	28	13	19
TACAIR	2	4			4	14	8	6	2		6	27	19	16	1	9	1	2	2	1	4	4
U.S. TOTAL	33	30	27	15	6	29	36	100	34	50	90	93	119	91	80	87	88	90	70	175	92	77

SOURCE: 7AF (DOA)

MR II FLOWN SORTIES   APR - MAY 1972

	20	21	22	23	24	25	26	27	28	29	30	1	2	3	4	5	6	7	8	9
VNAF	42	35	37	42	32	35	41	36	40	39	32	41	39	36	49	26	18	44	47	40
USMC	30	29	27	30	32	34	38	32	36	28	27	10	40	32	32	36	12	18	29	36
USN	31	4	55	37	76	52	77	12	8		53	25	18	10	19	36	8	3	2	14
ARC LIGHT	15	30	21	30	36	39	26	27	39	33	39	25	24	38	22	36	18	27	27	30
GUNSHIPS	6	5	5	3	10	6	8	8	7	8	3	3	6	2	5	5	5	5	5	4
TACAIR	3	13	25	35	53	76	75	34	36	18	44	42	48	49	40	19	19	8	12	26
U.S. TOTAL	85	81	133	135	207	207	224	113	126	87	166	105	136	131	118	96	62	61	75	110

SOURCE: 7AF (DOA)

MR II FLOWN SORTIES MAY 1972

	10	11	12	13	14	15	16	17	18	19	20	21	22	23	24	25	26	27	28	29	30	31
VNAF	41	39	13	38	55	38	49	43	47	38	64	48	49	48	43	44	59	38	44	48	34	23
USMC	32	33	29	18	30	29	33	10	10	12	24	22	14	8	16	14	10	19	18	8	14	14
USN		6	4			3									1			18			25	11
ARC LIGHT	34	9	51	6	33	35	24	36	48	45	40	36	33	41	27	29	47	54	36	54	51	30
GUNSHIPS	5	6	4	5	2	4	3	3	4	3	1	3	3	3	2	4	6	5	7	1	5	5
TACAIR	22	12	17	21	19	45	26	30	28	50	50	56	48	53	35	46	68	82	91	86	69	87
U.S. TOTAL	93	66	105	50	84	122	88	79	90	110	115	117	98	105	81	93	131	178	152	149	164	147

SOURCE: 7AF (DOA)

MR II FLOWN SORTIES   JUNE 1972

	1	2	3	4	5	6	7	8	9	10	11	12	13	14	15	16	17	18	19	20	21	22	23	24	25	26	27	28	29	30
VNAF	36	39	15	6	7	11	16	15	30	24	28	25	29	44	33	41	39	24	33	41	41	65	40	23	38	40	26	27	26	24
USMC	16	14	8	24	10	16	15	16	16	4	8	4	8	8	4	6	6	8	10	2	-	-	-	-	-	-	-	-	-	2
USN	-	-	-	-	50	20	-	-	48	24	35	28	52	56	67	57	30	38	19	14	23	17	2	2	-	13	-	-	-	-
ARC LIGHT	21	24	12	35	20	36	56	24	23	14	17	23	7	9	12	20	31	23	9	38	24	16	3	10	9	9	-	-	1	3
GUNSHIPS	1	5	3	3	3	2	2	3	4	4	4	5	4	2	4	3	3	3	2	1	2	1	4	3	4	3	4	1	1	2
TACAIR	40	70	71	64	68	92	88	70	78	43	69	59	48	52	42	50	46	22	40	34	50	40	52	58	58	31	16	22	24	22
U.S. TOTAL	78	113	94	126	151	166	161	113	169	89	133	119	119	127	129	136	116	94	80	89	99	74	61	73	71	56	20	26	26	29

SOURCE: 7AF (DOA/SEADAB)

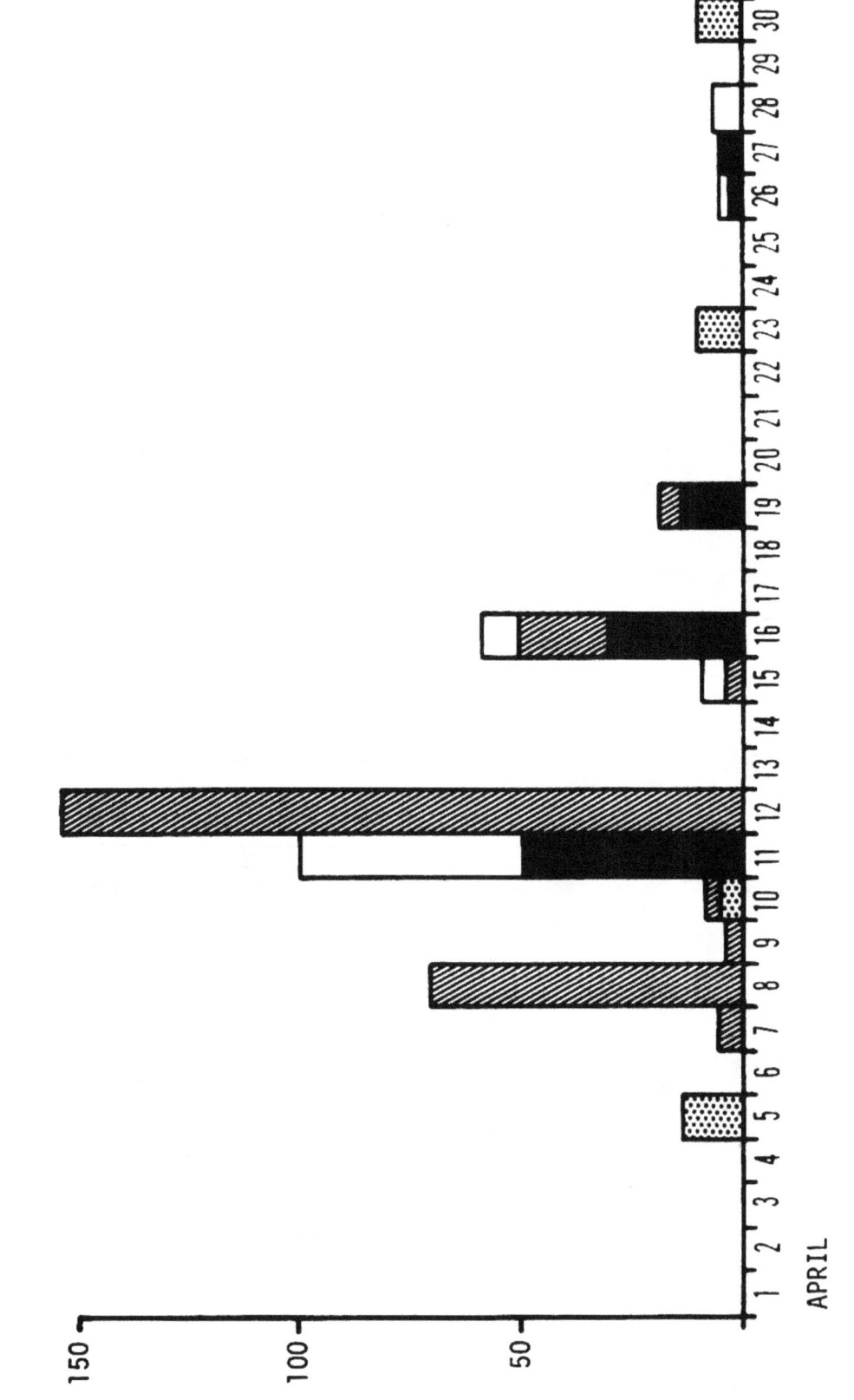

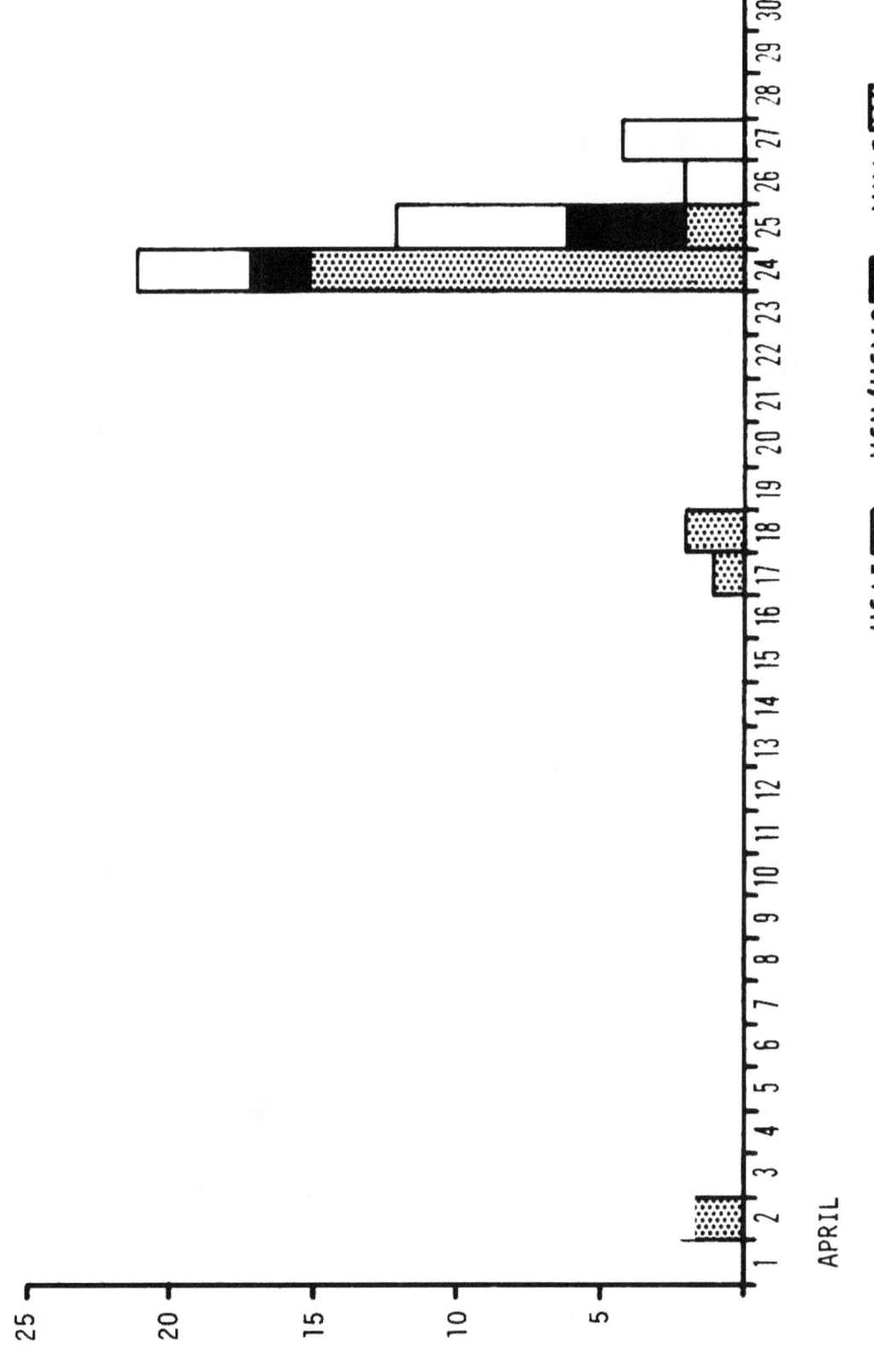

MR II TRUCKS DES/DAM - APRIL

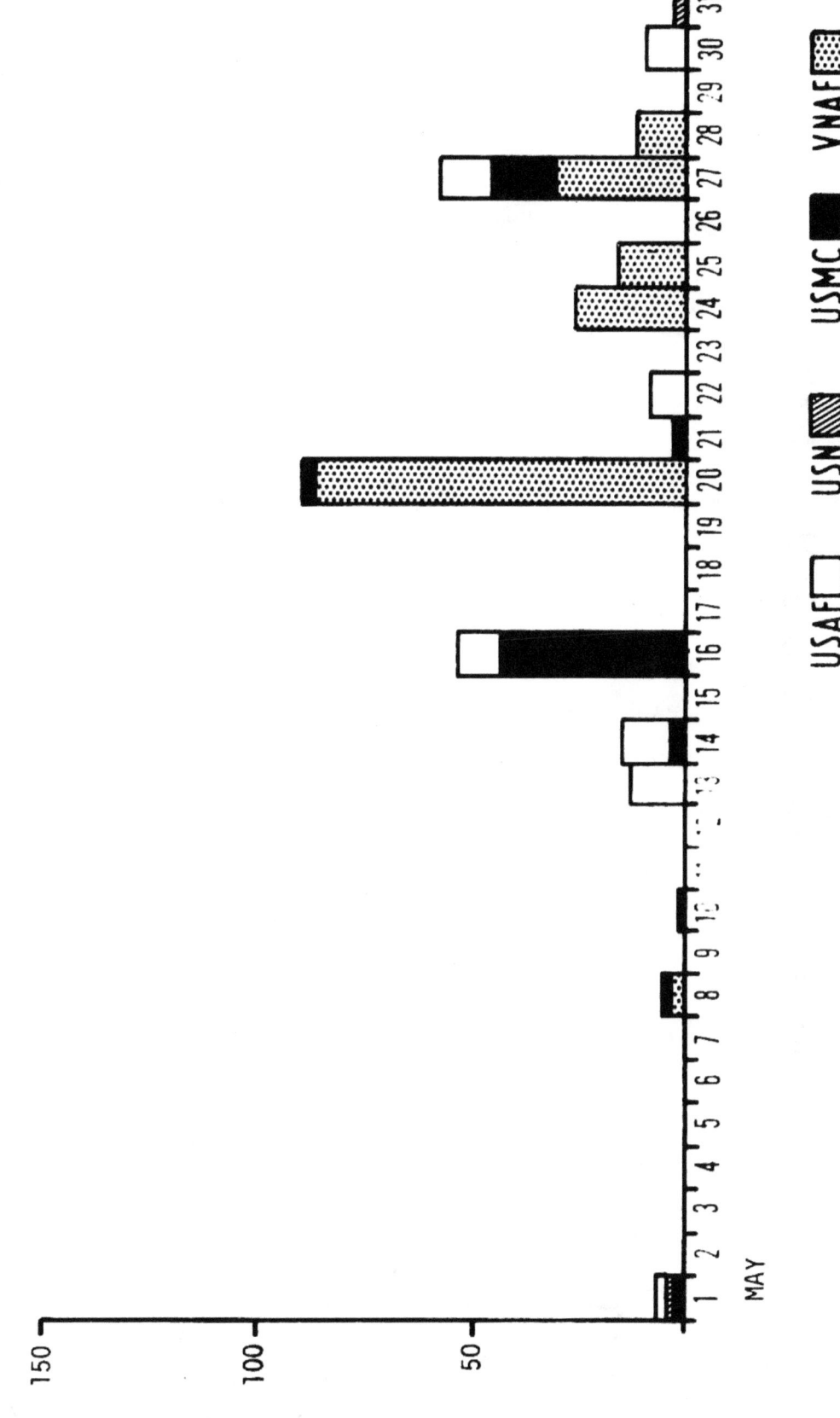

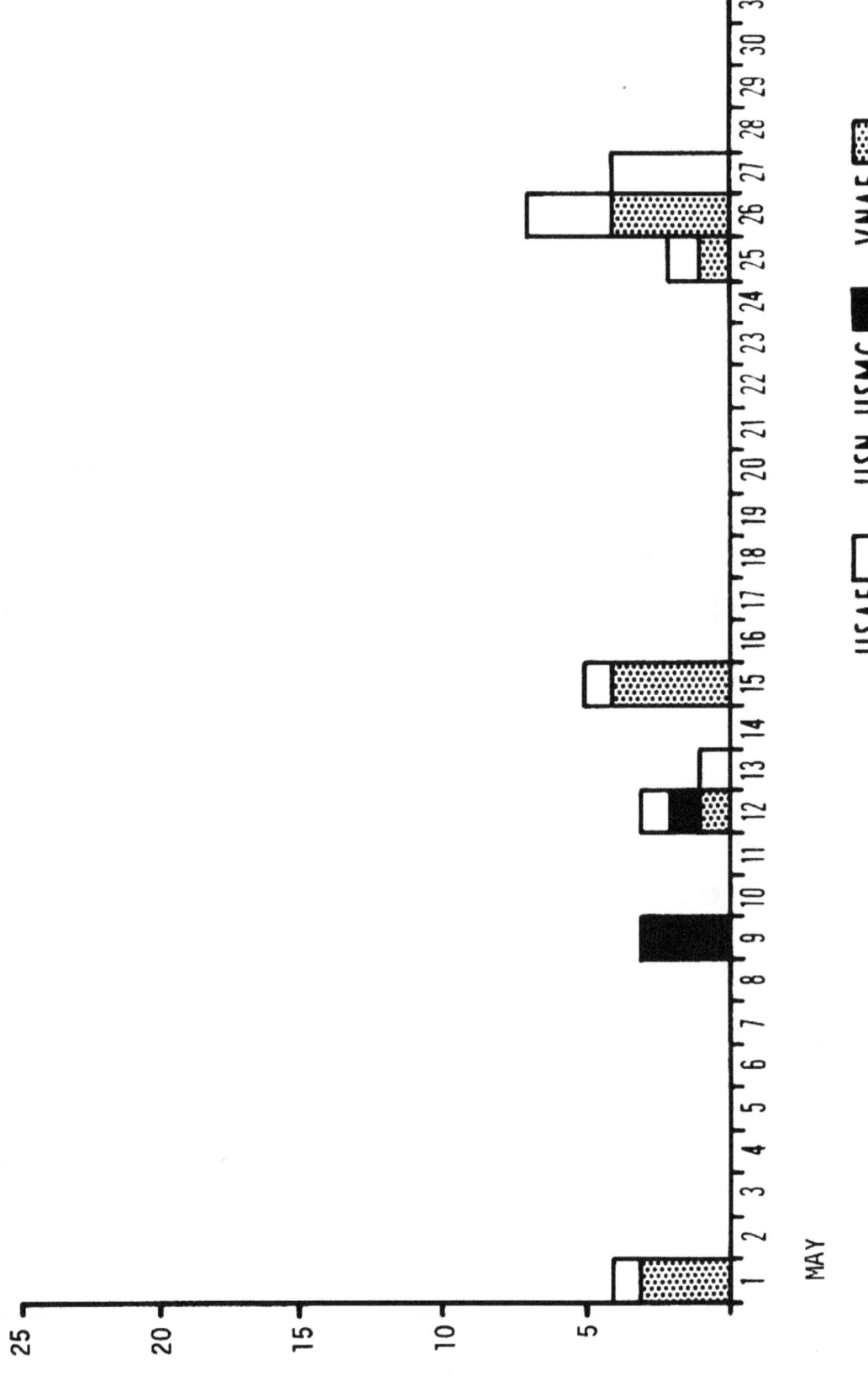

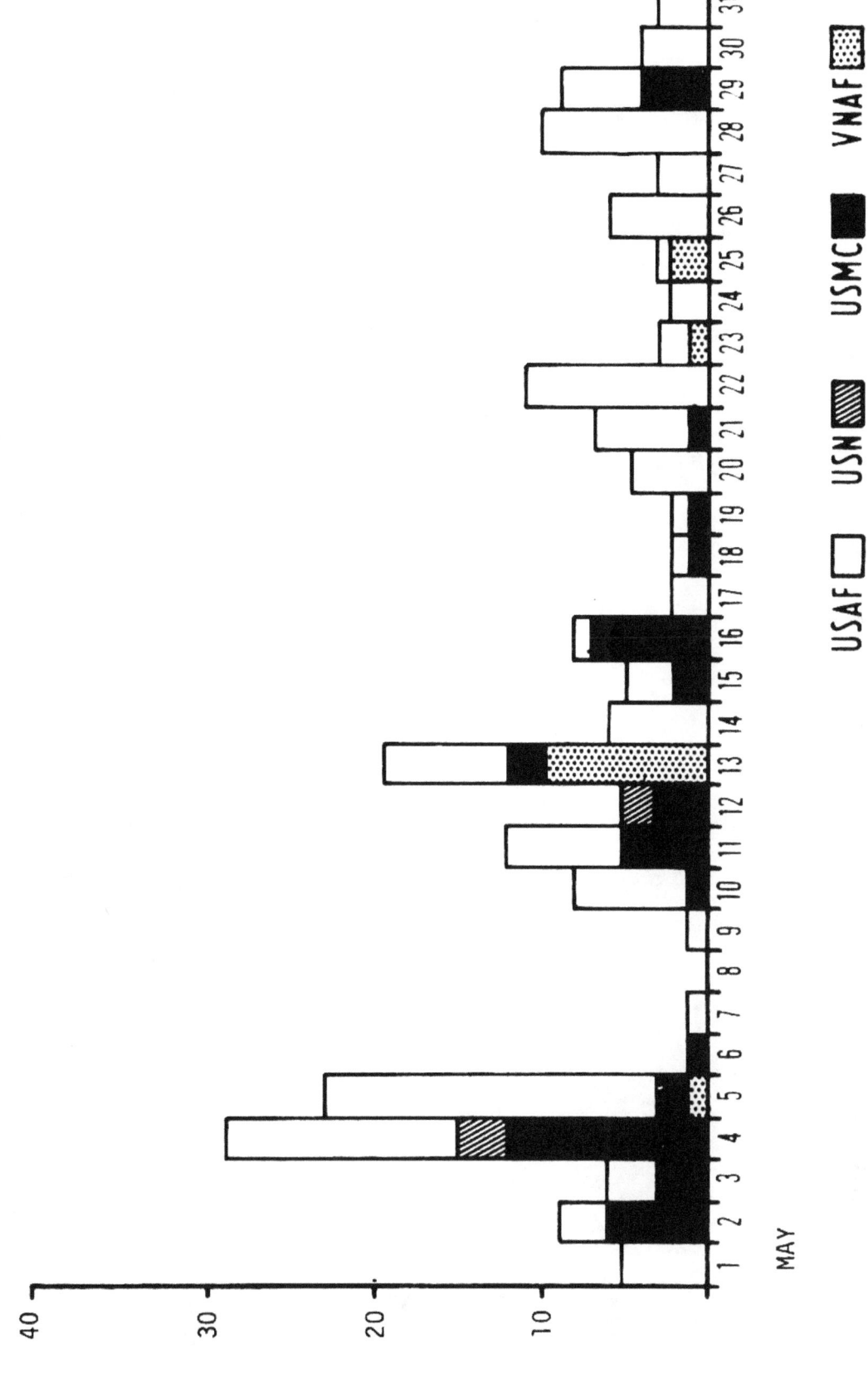

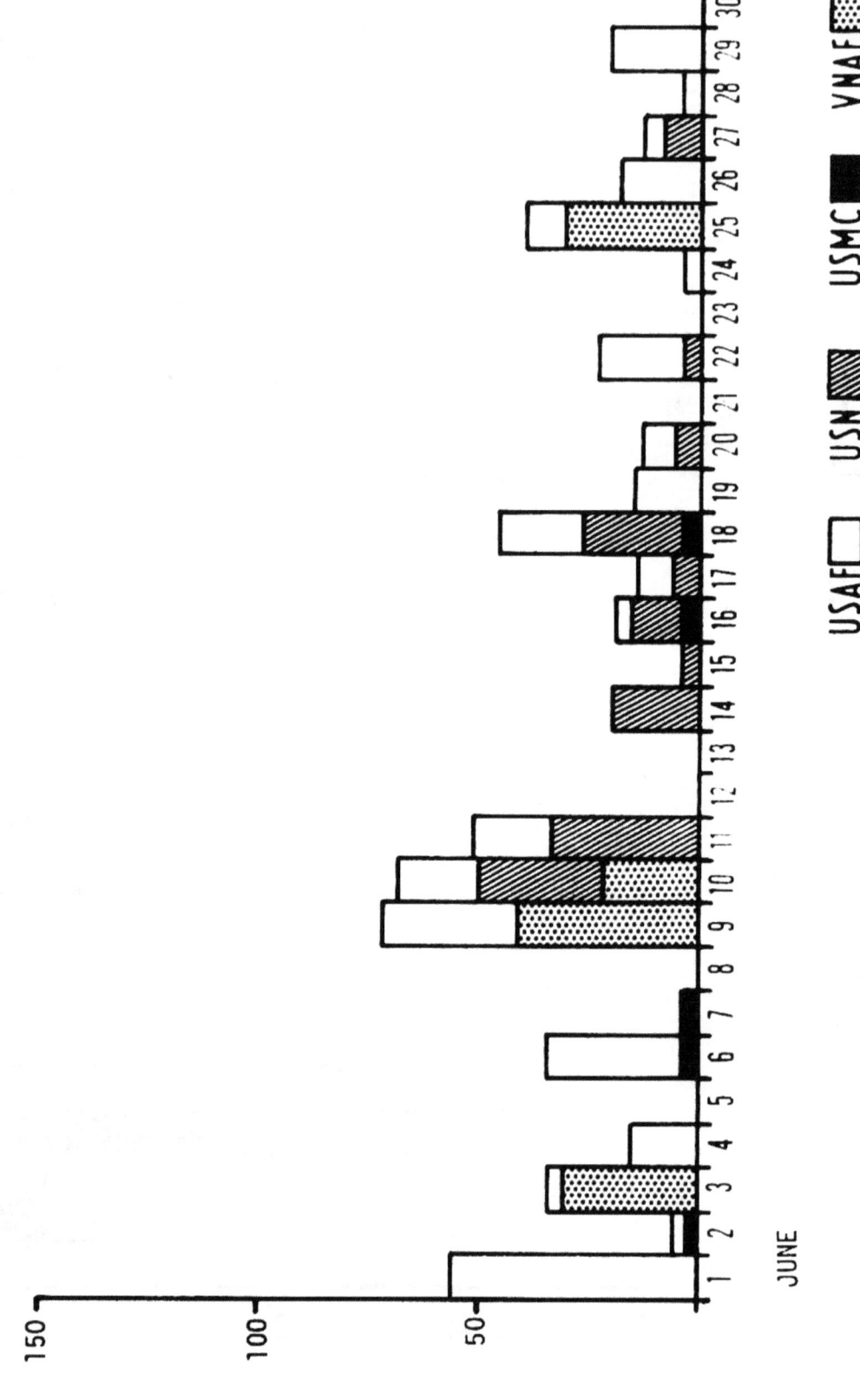

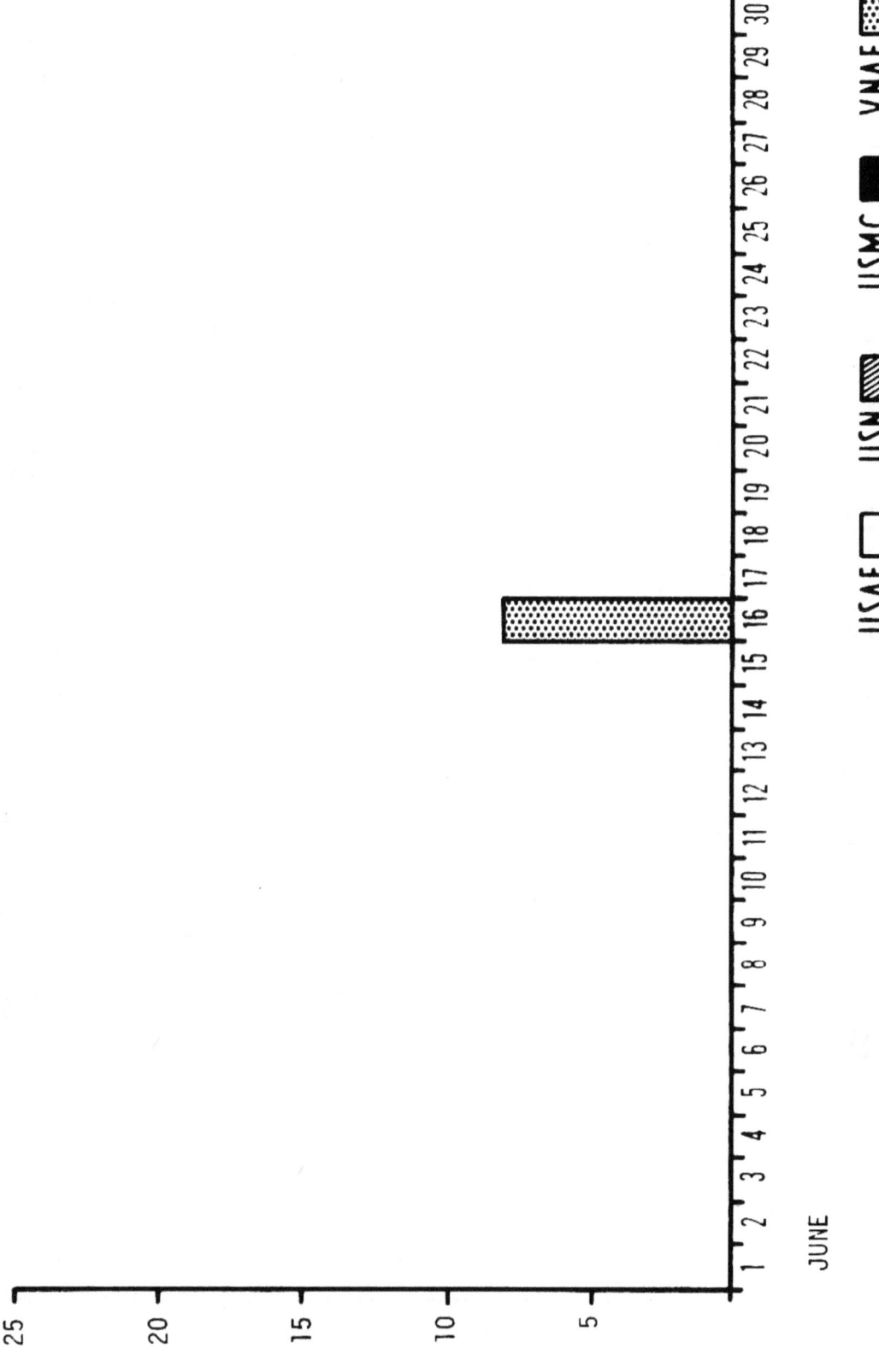

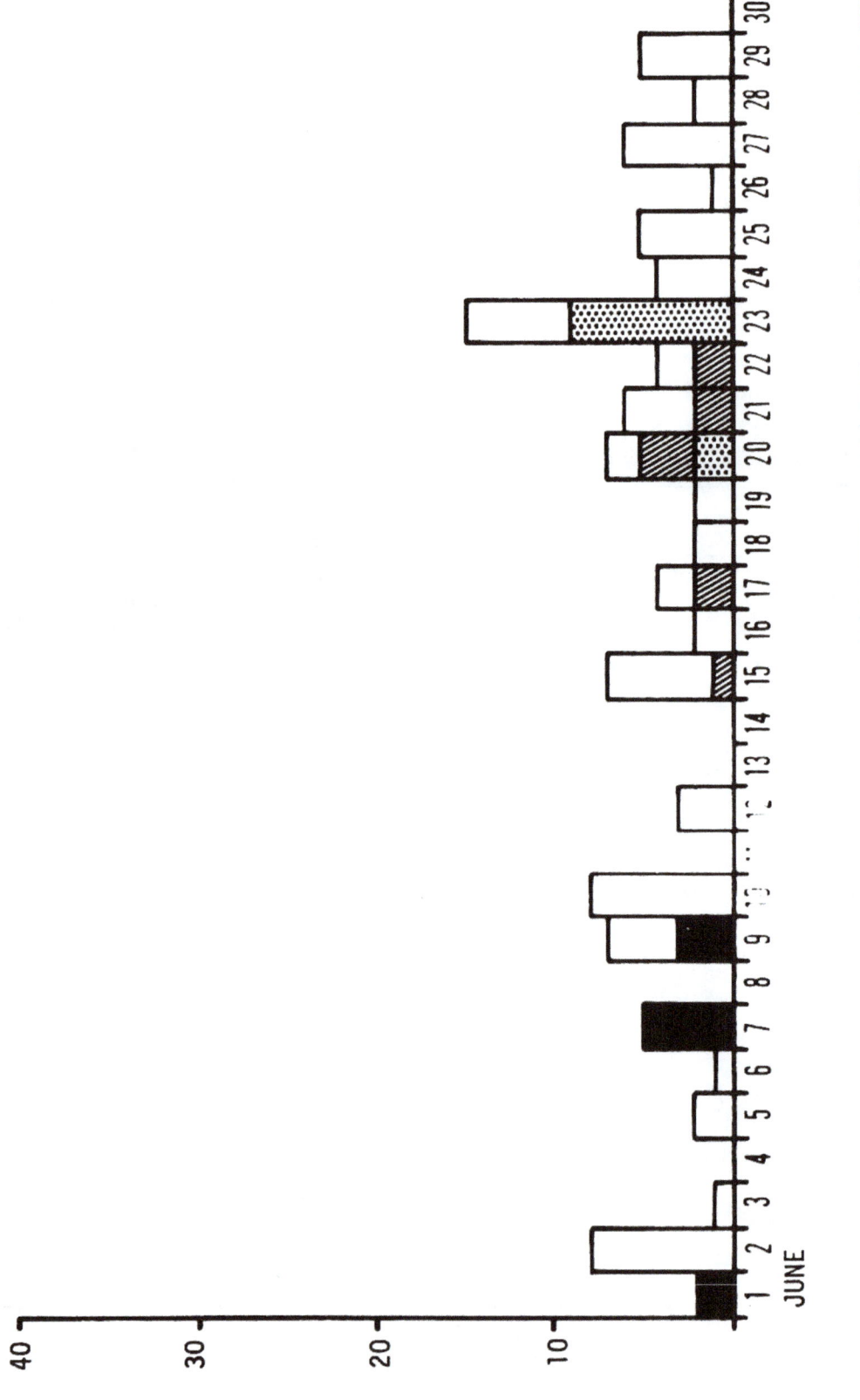

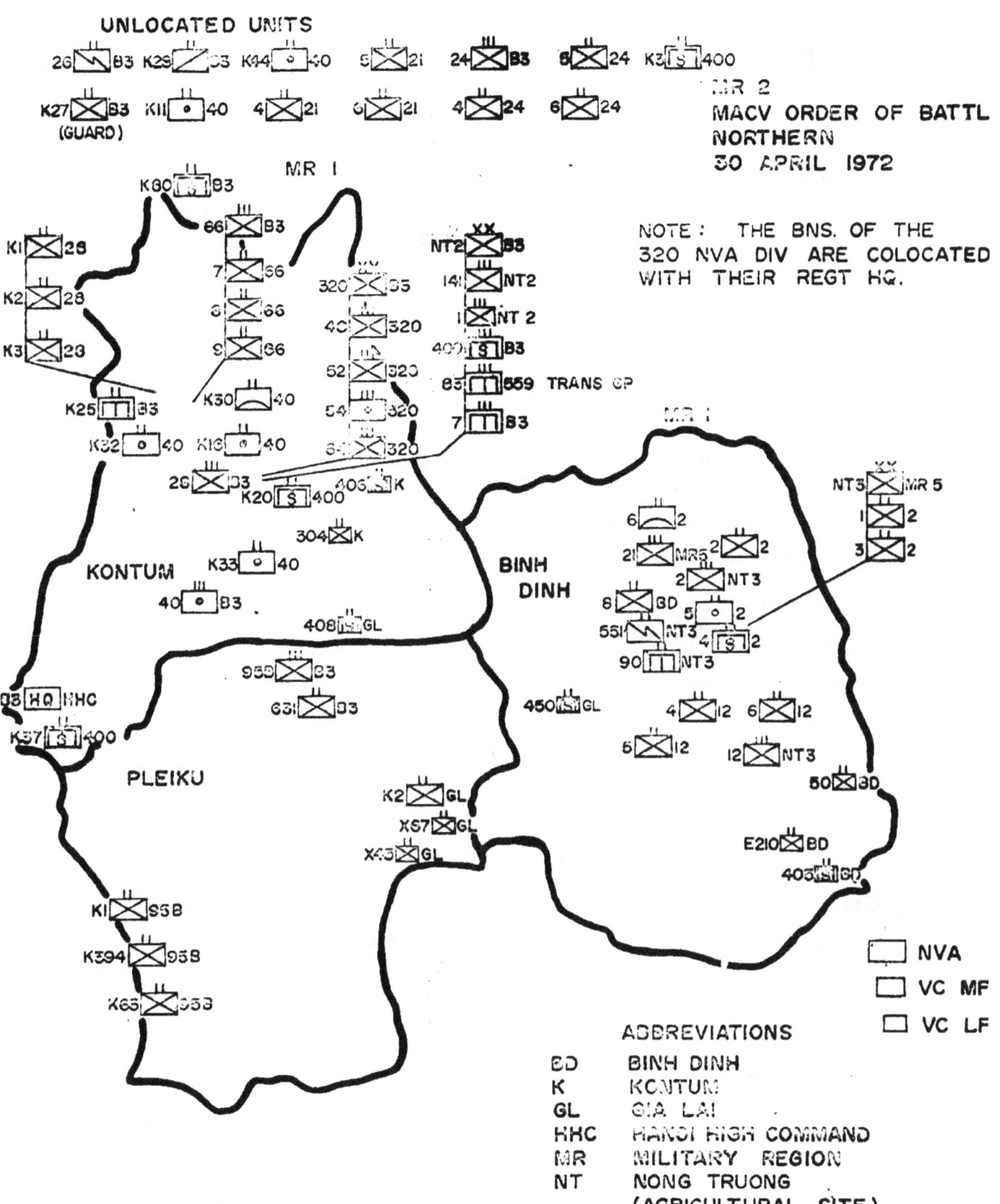

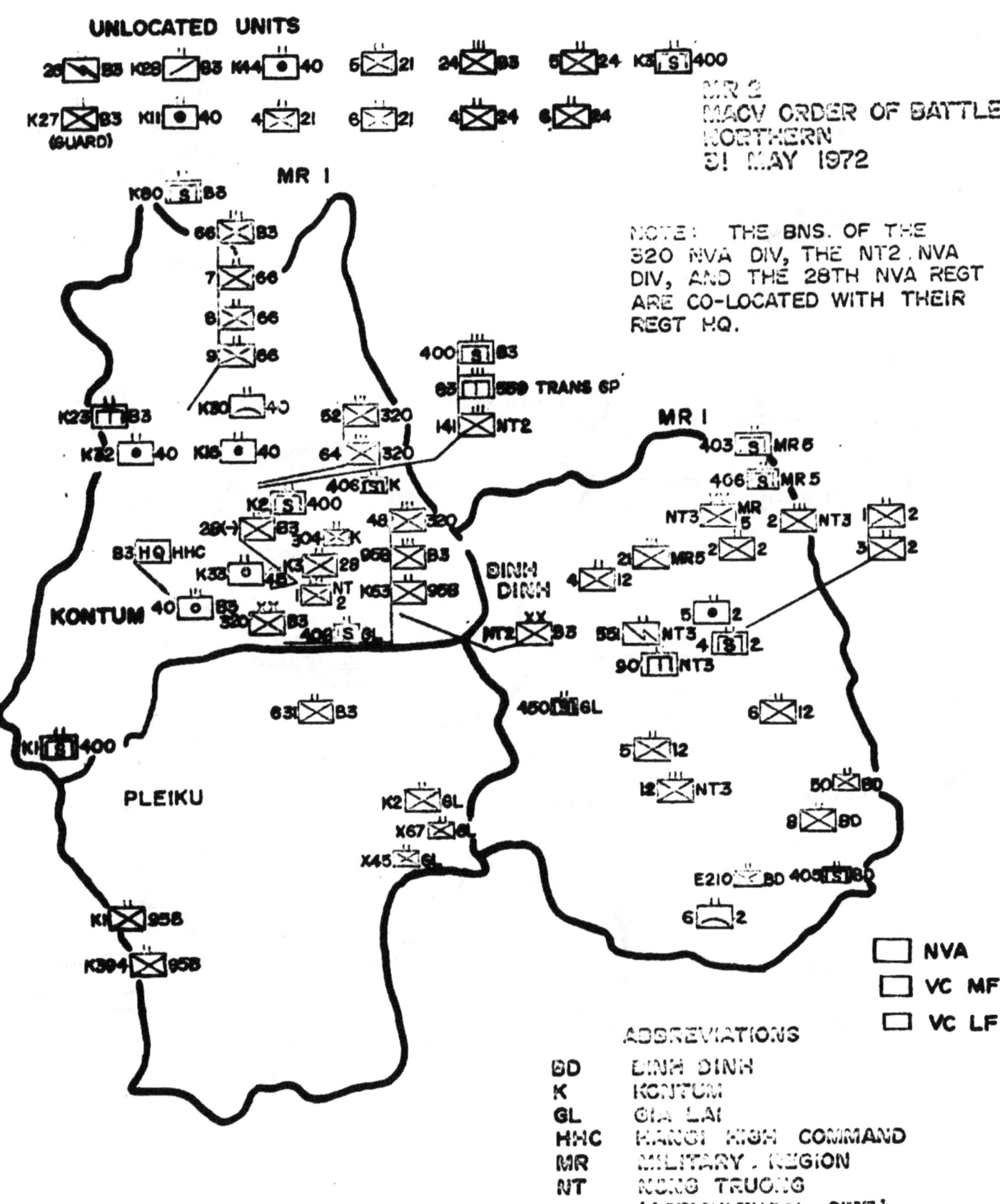

FOOTNOTES

1. (TS/AFEO) Seventh Air Force Intelligence Position Paper, prepared 8 Jun 72 by Lt Col A. Washington, Lt Robert D. Clifton, Capt Charles A. Nicholson and Capt Peter A. W. Liebchen for Project CHECO. Hereafter cited as (TS/AFEO) 7th AF Intelligence Paper. NOTE: Portions of the Position Paper cited in this study do not carry a security classification higher than Secret/Noforn.

2. (S/NF) Working Paper, MACV J-2, "The Highlands Campaign - Defense of Kontum City," May 72, p. 1. Hereafter cited as (S/NF) MACV J-2 Working Paper.

3. (S/NF) Ibid., p. 2.

4. (S/NF) Interview, 23 Jun 1972, Capt Peter A. W. Liebchen, Project CHECO, with Capt Steven Hicks, USAF, FAC, acting Air Liaison Officer (ALO) of the Covey FAC Detachment at Pleiku. Hereafter cited as the Hicks Interview.

5. (S/NF) Interview, 15 Jun 72, Capt Peter A. W. Liebchen, Project CHECO, with Lt John J. Kittle, USAF, Covey FAC, 20th TASS. Hereafter cited as the Kittle Interview.

6. (S/NF) Ibid.

7. (S/NF) Interview, 22 Jun 72, Capt Peter A. W. Liebchen, Project CHECO, with Major Jerry Gerlitz, USAF, Senior Fighter Duty Officer, II DASC, Pleiku. Hereafter cited as the Gerlitz Interview.

8. (S/NF) MACV J-2 Working Paper, p. 1.

9. (S/NF) Ibid.

10. (TS/AFEO) 7th AF Intelligence Position Paper. Portion cited is S/NF in classification.

11. (S/NF) Prepared briefing by Lt Col James W. Bricker, USAF, Senior Advisor G-3 Section to the ARVN 23d Division. Also Deputy Forward Division Advisor, Kontum City. Hereafter cited as G-3 Briefing.

12.	(S/NF)	MACV J-2 Working Paper, p. 2.
13.	(S/NF)	Interview, 20 Jun 72, Capt Peter A. W. Liebchen, Project CHECO, with Major William Damon, USA, Air Mobile Advisor to II Corps, Pleiku. Hereafter referred to as the Damon Interview.
14.	(TS/AFEO)	7th AF Intelligence Position Paper. Portion cited is S/NF in classification.
15.	(S/NF)	MACV J-2 Working Paper, p. 2.
16.	(S/NF)	Ibid.
17.	(S/NF)	CAS Daily Vietnam Situation Reports, FVS 29,163, 2 Apr 72. Hereafter cited as CAS Report with appropriate FVS number.
18.	(S/NF)	7th AF Daily Intelligence Briefing, 3 Apr 72. Hereafter cited as 7AF, DIB.
19.	(S/NF)	7AF, DIB, 4 Apr 72.
20.	(S/NF)	CAS Report, FVS 29,171, 4 Apr 72.
21.	(S/NF)	CAS Report, FVS 29,177, 4 Apr 72.
22.	(S/NF)	Ibid.
23.	(S/NF)	CAS Report, FVS 29,197, 5 Apr 72.
24.	(S/NF)	CAS Report, FVS 29,203, 6 Apr 72.
25.	(S/NF)	CAS Report, FVS 29,214, 7 Apr 72, FVS 29,216/29, 228, 8 Apr 72.
26.	(S/NF)	MACV J-2 Working Paper, May 72, p. 3.
27.	(S/NF)	7th AF: DIB, 8 Apr 72.
28.	(S/NF)	CAS Report, FVS 29,231, 9 Apr 72, p. 3.
29.	(S/NF)	CAS Report, FVS 29,251, 12 Apr 72, p. 5.
30.	(S/NF)	7th AF, DIB, 9 Apr 72.

31. (S/NF)   CAS Report, FVS 29,231, 9 Apr 72.
32. (S/NF)   Ibid.
33. (S/NF)   MACV J-2 Working Paper, May 72, p. 3.
34. (S/NF)   7th AF: DIB, 13 Apr 72.
35. (S/NF)   Ibid.
36. (S/NF)   CAS Report, FVS 29,299, 15 Apr 72.
37. (S/NF)   MACV J-2 Working Paper, May 72, p. 3.
38. (U)   Pacific Stars and Stripes, 21 Apr 72, p. 7.
39. (S/NF)   CAS Report, FVS 29,244, 10 Apr 72, p. 2.
40. (S/NF)   CAS Report, FVS 29,290, 15 Apr 72 and FVS 29,358, 20 Apr 72.
41. (S/NF)   CAS Report, FVS 29,284, 14 Apr 72.
42. (S/NF)   7th AF: DIB, 20 Apr 72.
43. (C)   Gunship Operational Summary, Stinger 12, Mission #5248, 21 Apr 72. 18th SOS, Nakhon Phanom RTAFB. Hereafter cited as Stinger Operational Summary.
44. (S/NF)   MACV J-2 Working Paper, May 72, p. 4.
45. (S/NF)   CAS Report, FVS 29,387, 22 Apr 72.
46. (S/NF)   CAS Report, FVS 29,382, 22 Apr 72.
47. (C)   AC-130 Mission Report, Spectre 08, Mission #5236, 21 Apr 72, 16th SOS, Ubon RTAFB. Hereafter cited as AC-130 Mission Report.
48. (S/NF)   MACV J-2 Working Paper, May 72, p. 4.
49. (S/NF)   CAS Report, FVS 29,395, 23 Apr 72.
50. (S/NF)   7AF, DIB, 24 Apr 72, p. 6.

51. (S/NF)   Ibid.

52. (C)   MACV Daily Log, 23/24 Apr 72, pp. 5, 6.

53. (S/NF)   7AF, DIB, 24 Apr 72, p. 7.

54. (U)   AF Form 642, 8 Jun 72, 16SOS, Ubon RTAFB. Recommendation for Silver Star, Capt Russel J. Olson, 502-48-8198FV.

55. (S)   16 SOS Quarterly History (Draft), Mar-Jun 72, pp. 1-4.

56. (C)   MACV Daily Log 23/24 Apr 72, p. 6.

57. (C)   MACV Daily Log 23/24 Apr 72, p. 7.

58. (S/NF)   7AF, Day Mission Summary, 24 Apr 72, p. 3.

59. (C)   MACV Daily Log, 23/24 Apr 72, pp. 8-12.

60. (S/NF)   Hicks Interview.

61. (S/NF)   Interview, 20 Jun 72, Capt Peter A. W. Liebchen, Project CHECO, with Lt Col Lee A. Goff, USA, SRAG TOC G-3, Pleiku. Hereafter cited as Goff Interview.

62. (S/NF)   Ibid.

63. (S/NF)   Interview, 22 Jun 72, Capt Peter A. W. Liebchen, Project CHECO, with Major Gordon E. Bloom, USAF, Asst II Corps ALO advisor to the VNAF, II DASC. Hereafter cited as the Bloom Interview.

64. (S/NF)   Bricker Interview.

65. (S/NF)   Bloom Interview.

66. (S/NF)   Goff Interview.

67. (S/NF)   7th AF, DIB, 24-26 Apr 72.

68. (S/NF)   Gerlitz Interview.

69. (S/NF)   CAS Report, FVS 29,455, 28 Apr 72.

70. (S/NF)   Gerlitz Interview.

71.	(C)	AC-130 Mission Report, Spectre 05, Mission #5218, 27 Apr 72.
	(C)	AC-130 Mission Report, Spectre 19, Mission #5218, 25 Apr 72.
72.	(S/NF)	7th AF, Night Mission Summary, 25 Apr 72, p. 3.
73.	(S/NF)	7th AF, DIB, 27 Apr 72.
74.	(C)	AC-130 Mission Report, Spectre 10, Mission #5239, 26 Apr 72.
75.	(S/NF)	G-3 Briefing (Lt Col James W. Bricker, USA).
76.	(S/NF)	Bloom Interview.
77.	(S/NF)	CAS Report, FVS 29,412, 24 Apr 72.
78.	(S/NF)	CAS Report, FVS 29,470, 28 Apr 72.
79.	(S/NF)	7AF, DIB, 27 Apr 72, p. 7.
80.	(S/NF)	7AF, DIB, 30 Apr 72.
81.	(S/NF)	CAS Report, FVS 29,478/29,488, 29/30 Apr 72.
82.	(S/NF)	7AF, DIB, 2 May, p. 6.
83.	(S/NF)	Interview, 20 Jun 72, Capt Peter A. W. Liebchen, Project CHECO, with Capt Thomas K. Ellis, USAF, Air Intelligence Officer, II DASC, Pleiku. Hereafter cited as the Ellis Interview.
84.	(S/NF)	Gerlitz Interview.
85.	(S/NF)	Ibid.
86.	(C)	Msg, II DASC to 7AF/DO, 011000Z May 72, p. 1.
87.	(C)	Ibid.
88.	(C)	Msg, II DASC to 7AF/DO, 020910Z May 72.
89.	(C)	Msg, II DASC to 7AF/DO, 011000Z May 72, pp. 2-3.
90.	(C)	Msg, II DASC to 7AF/DO, 020910Z May 72, p. 1.

91. (C)   Msg, II DASC to 7AF/DO, 020910Z May 72, pp. 203.

92. (C)   Msg, II DASC to 7AF/DO, 031358Z May 72, p. 1.

93. (C)   Ibid.

94. (S)   Msg, II DASC to 7AF/DO, 040833Z May 72.

95. (S/LIMDIS) Msg, II DASC to 7AF/CC, 050630Z May 72.

96. (S/NF)   CAS Report, FVS 29,582, 6 May 72.

97. (S)   Msg, II DASC to 7AF/DO, 050920Z May 72.

98. (S)   Msgs, II DASC to 7AF/DO, 050920Z/052000Z May 72.

99. (S)   Msgs, II DASC to 7AF/DO, 061944Z/062000Z May 72.

100. (S/NF)   CAS Report, FVS 7 May 72.

101. (S)   Msgs, II DASC to 7AF/DO, 072005Z/080910Z May 72.

102. (S/NF)   MACV J-2 Working Paper, May 72, p. 6.

103. (S)   Msgs, II DASC to 7AF/DO, 080912Z/082010Z/082130Z May 72.

104. (S)   Msgs, II DASC to 7AF/DO, 090755Z/100400Z May 72.

105. (S)   Msg, II DASC to 7AF/DO, 100843Z May 72.

106. (S/NF)   CAS Report, FVS 29,638, 10 May 72.

107. (S/NF)   Ibid.

108. (S/NF)   Bricket Interview.

109. (S)   Msg, II DASC to 7AF/DO, 102000Z May 72.

110. (S)   Msgs, II DASC to 7AF/DO, 110851Z/112201Z May 72.

111. (S)   Msg, II DASC to 7AF/DO, 120734Z May 72.

112. (S/NF)   Bricker Interview.

113. (S)   Msgs, II DASC to 7AF/DO, 130839Z/132020Z May 72.
114. (S/NF)   CAS Report, FVS 29,683, 14 May 72.
115. (S/NF)   Bricker Interview.
116. (C)   Msgs, II DASC to 7AF/DO, 140845Z/142000Z May 72.
117. (S/NF)   Interview, 21 Jun 72, Capt Peter A. W. Liebchen with Colonel Rothenberry, USA, Senior Advisor to ARVN 23d Division, Kontum City. Hereafter cited as Rothenberry Interview.
118. (S/NF)   CAS Report, FVS 29,707, 15 May 72.
119. (S/NF)   7AF, DIB, 15 May 72.
120. (S)   Msg, II DASC to 7AF/DO, 170930Z May 72.
121. (C)   Msgs, II DASC to 7AF/DO, 150950Z/150320Z/152000Z May 72.
122. (C)   Msgs, II DASC to 7AF/DO, 160800Z/162000Z May 72.
123. (S/NF)   CAS Report, FVS 29,711, 16 May 72.
124. (S/NF)   7th AF, DIB, 18 May 72, p. 5.
125. (S)   Msg, II DASC to 7AF/DO, 170930Z May 72.
126. (S/NF)   Rothenberry Interview.
127. (C)   Msg, Director SRAG to COMUSMACV, Subj: Intelligence Update in Connection with Daily Commanders Evaluation, 19 May 72. Hereafter cited as SRAG Intelligence Update.
128. (S/NF)   CAS Report, FVS 29,749, 19 May 72, p. 3.
129. (S)   Msg, II DASC to 7AF/DO, 202010Z May 72. Also SRAG Daily Commander's Evaluation for 24 hours, 20 May 72.
130. (C)   SRAG Intelligence Update, 19 May 72.
131. (S)   Msg, II DASC to 7AF/DO, 212025Z May 72.
132. (S)   Msg, II DASC to 7AF/DO, 220850Z May 72.

133. (S) Msg, II DASC to 7AF/DO, 222030Z May 72. Also SRAG Intelligence Update 22/23 May 72.

134. (S) 16th SOS Quarterly History (Draft), Mar-Jun 72, pp. 1-51.

135. (C) Daily Staff Journal/Duty Officers Log, USAFF Compound, 23d ARVN OTOC: Kontum City. Hereafter cited as Daily Staff Journal.

136. (C) SRAG Intelligence Update, 24 May 72.

137. (S) Msg, II DASC to 7AF/DO, 23/24 May 72.

138. (S) Msg, II DASC to 7AF/DO, 240920Z May 72. Also SRAG Intelligence Update, 24 May 72.

139. (S/NF) G-3 Briefing (Lt Col James W. Bricker, USA) and Daily Staff Journal, 25 May 72.

140. (S/NF) G-3 Briefing (Lt Col James W. Bricker, USA).

141. (S) Msg, II DASC to 7AF/DO: 250847Z May 72 also SRAG, Daily Commanders Evaluation, 25 May 72.

142. (S) Ibid.

143. (S/NF) G-3 Briefing (Lt Col James W. Bricker, USA).

144. (S) Msg, II DASC to 7AF/DO, 260930Z May 72. Also Daily Staff Journal, 26 May 72.

145. (S) Msgs, II DASC to 7AF/DO, 260930Z May 72, also Daily Staff Journal, 26 May 72.

146. (S) Msg, II DASC to 7AF/DO, 270855Z May 72.

147. (S) Msgs, II DASC to 7AF/DO, 270855Z/280415Z May 72.

148. (S/NF) Bloom Interview.

149. (S/NF) 7th AF, DIB, 28 May 72, p. 2.

150. (S/NF) Interview, 23 Jun 72, Capt Peter A. W. Liebchen, Project CHECO, with Col Joseph Pizzi, USA, Chief of Staff, HQ SRAG, Pleiku City. Hereafter cited as the Pizzi Interview.

151. (S)   Msgs., II DASC to 7AF/DO, 280952Z/282040Z May 72.
152. (S/NF) 7th AF, DIB, 28 May 72.
153. (S)   Msg., II DASC to 7AF/DO, 290220Z May 72.
154. (S)   Ibid.
155. (S)   Msgs., II DASC to 7AF/DO, 290935Z/29/30 May 72.
156. (S)   Msg., II DASC to 7AF/DO, 302110Z May 72.
157. (S)   Msg., II DASC to 7AF/DO, 310935Z May 72.
158. (S)   Ibid.
159. (S)   Msg., II DASC to 7AF/DO, 010700Z Jun 72.
160. (S)   Msg., II DASC to 7AF/DO, 021030Z Jun 72.
161. (S)   Ibid.
162. (S/NF) 7th AF, DIB, 3 Jun 72.
163. (S)   Msgs., II DASC to 7AF/DO, 030945Z/032030Z Jun 72. Also 7th AF, DIB, 3 Jun 72.
164. (S)   Msgs., II DASC to 7AF/DO, 040345Z/042020Z Jun 72.
165. (S)   Msgs., II DASC to 7AF/DO, 050915Z/5/6 Jun 72.
166. (S/NF) 7th AF, DIB, 6 Jun 72, p. 3.
167. (S)   Msgs., II DASC to 7AF/DO, 060545Z/060730Z Jun 72.
168. (S)   Msg., II DASC to 7AF/DO, 061000Z Jun 72.
169. (S)   Msg., II DASC to 7AF/DO 070850Z Jun 72.
170. (S)   Ibid.
171. (S)   Ibid.

172.	(S)	Msg., II DASC to 7AF/DO, 080940Z Jun 72.
173.	(S)	Msg., II DASC to 7AF/DO, 081125Z Jun 72.
174.	(S)	Ibid.
175.	(S)	Msg., II DASC to 7AF/DO, 091800Z, 9/10 Jun 72.
176.	(S)	Msg., II DASC to 7AF/DO, 100950Z Jun 72.
177.	(S/NF)	Goff Interview.
178.	(S/NF)	Rothenberry Interview.
179.	(S/NF)	Hicks Interview.
180.	(S/NF)	Interview, 21 Jun 72, Capt Peter A. W. Liebchen, Project CHECO, with Brigadier General Ba, Commander, 23d ARVN Division, Kontum City.
181.	(C)	Msg., COMUSMACV to 8th AF, Guam, 150851Z May 72.
182.	(S)	Msg., II DASC to 7AF/DO, 050920Z May 72.
183.	(S/NF)	Hicks Interview.
184.	(C)	AC-130 Mission Report, Spectre 19, Mission #5201, 2 May 72.
185.	(C)	AC-130 Mission Report, Spectre 15, Mission #5211, 6 May 72.
186.	(S/NF)	Hicks Interview.
187.	(C)	AC-130 Mission Report Spectre 19, Mission #5214, 9 May 72.
188.	(S)	Msg., 7AF to 8 TFW, 010330Z May 72.
189.	(S)	Msg., II DASC to 7AF/TACC, Subj: Summary of U.S. Air Support MR II, 22 May-30 Jun 72.
190.	(C)	Msg., II DASC to 7AF/CV and 7AF/DO, Subj: Vehicle BDA, 100810Z May 72.
191.	(S/NF)	Ellis Interview.

192.	(C)	Daily Commander's Evaluation for 24 Hours, 210210Z May 72.
193.	(S)	16th SOS Quarterly History (Draft) Apr-Jun 72, pp. 1-25.
194.	(S)	Msg., II DASC to 7AF/DO, 110830Z Jun 72, and Interview, 31 Aug 72, Major Paul T. Ringenbach with Col D. B. Swenholt.
195.	(S)	16th SOS Quarterly History (Draft) Apr-Jun 72, pp. 1035.
196.	(S)	Msg., II DASC to 7AF/DO, 140930Z Jun 72.
197.	(S/NF)	Bloom Interview.
198.	(S/NF)	Demon Interview.
199.	(S/NF)	Rothenberry Interview.
200.	(S/NF)	Bloom Interview.
201.	(S/NF)	Pizzi Interview.
202.	(S/NF)	CAS Report FVS 30,210, 1 Jul 72. Subj: Appraisal of Situation. The VC/NVA Offensive At The End of Three Months. Hereafter cited as CAS Three Month Appraisal.
203.	(S/NF)	Bricker Interview.
204.	(S/NF)	Pizzi Interview.
205.	(S/NF)	Goff Interview.
206.	(S/NF)	Ibid.
207.	(S/NF)	Pizzi Interview.
208.	(U)	Article by George McArthur copyright 1972 by the Los Angeles Times. Reprinted by Pacific Stars and Stripes, Jul 23, 72, p. 11.
209.	(S/NF)	CAS Three Month Appraisal.
210.	(S/NF)	Hicks Interview.

GLOSSARY

AAA	Anti-Aircraft Artillery
ABF	Attack by Fire
ALO	Air Liaison Officer
AO	Area of Operations
ARVN	Army, Republic of Vietnam
BDA	Bomb Damage Assessment
B/G	Brigadier General
BN	Battalion
CAS	Controled American Source
CBU	Cluster Bomb Unit
CC	Command and Control
CO	Commanding Officer
CP	Command Post
CSS	COMBAT SKY SPOT
DASC	Direct Air Support Center
DIV	Division
DMZ	Demilitarized Zone
FAC	Forward Air Controller
FSB	Fire Support Base
GCA	Ground Control Approach
HQ	Headquarters
IFR	Instrument Flight Rules
INS	Inertial Navigation System
IR	Infrared
JGS	Joint General Staff
KIA	Killed in Action
LAW	Light Anti-Tank Weapon
LGB	Laser Guided Bomb
LOC	Line of Communication
LOH	Light Observation Helicopter
LORAN	Long Range Airborne Navigation
LZ	Landing Zone

VC	Viet Cong
VFR	Visual Flight Rules
VNAF	South Vietnamese Air Force
VR	Visual Reconnaissance
WGM	Wire Guided Missile
WIA	Wounded in Action

MIA	Missing in Action
MSL	Mean Sea Level
MSQ	Mobile Search Special
MR	Military Region
NVA	North Vietnamese Army
NVN	North Vietnam
PF	Popular Force
POL	Petroleum, Oil and Lubricants
POW	Prisoner of War
REG	Regiment
RF	Regional Force
ROE	Rules of Engagement
ROK	Republic of Korea
RON	Remain Overnight
RTG	Return to Base
RVN	Republic of Vietnam
SAC	Strategic Air Command
SAM	Surface to Air Missile
SEX	Secondary Explosion
SOS	Special Operations Squadron
SRAG	Second Regional Assistance Group
TACAIR	Tactical Air
TACAN	Tactical Air Navigation
TACC	Tactical Air Control Center
TAC-E	Tactical Emergency
TACP	Tactical Air Control Party
TFW	Tactical Fighter Wing
TOC	Tactical Operations Center
TOT	Time on Target
TOW	Tube Launched, Optically Tracked, Wire-Guided Missile
USA	United States Army
USAF	United States Air Force
USMC	United States Marine Corps
USN	United States Navy

REPLY TO
ATTN OF: HO

17 January 1983

SUBJECT: Release of CHECO Documents

TO: AFSHRC/CC

1. The list of CHECO reports you sent to us with your letter of 3 January are releasable as far as PACAF Public Affairs are concerned. When referring to CHECO documents, it's most helpful if you include the number assigned in the Research Guide you published in 1976.

2. We will be sending you the Air America documents as soon as we can spare the time to pack them up--we need the vault space.

3. Am retiring at the end of this month, so you probably won't be hearing from me again. It's been nice knowing you and working with your very supportive organization. Best wishes for the future.

JAMES C. NOLAN
Chief, Office of PACAF History

UNCLASSIFIED/DECLASSIFIED CHECO REPORTS

1. Project RED HORSE (Unclassified), by Derek H. Willard, 1 Sep 1969   K717.0413-68

2. USAF Aerial Port Operations in RVN (Unclassified), by Jack T. Humphries, 5 Aug 1970   K717.0413-79

3. SEA Glossary 1961-1971 (Revised Report) (Unclassified), by E. J. Alsperger, 1 Feb 1972   K717.0413-76

4. OV-1/AC-119 Hunter-Killer Team (Declassified), by Richard R. Sexton and William M. Hodgson, 10 Oct 1972   K717.0413-34

5. Kontum: Battle for the Central Highlands 30 March-10 June 1972 (Declassified), by Peter Liebchen, 27 Oct 1972   K717.0414-30

6. PAVE MACE/COMBAT RENDEZVOUS (Declassified), by Richard R. Sexton, 26 Dec 1972   K717.0414-35

7. Air Defense in Southeast Asia 1945-1971 (Declassified), by Guyman Penix and Paul T. Ringenbach, 17 Jan 1973   K717.0414-36

8. The Battle for An Loc 5 April - 26 June 1972 (Declassified), by Paul T. Ringenbach and Peter J. Melly, 31 Jan 1973   K717.0414-31

9. PAVE AEGIS Weapon System (AC-130E Gunship) (Declassified), by Gerald J. Till and James C. Thomas, 16 Feb 1973   K717.0414-37

10. The 1972 Invasion of Military Region I: Fall of Quang Tri and Defense of Hue (Declassified), by David K. Mann, 15 Mar 1973   K717.0414-32

11. "Ink" Development and Employment (Declassified*), by B. H. Barnette, Jr., 24 Sep 1973   K717.0414-41

12. Guided Bomb Operations in SEA: The Weather Dimension 1 February - 31 December 1972 (Declassified), by Patrick J. Breitling, 1 Oct 1973   K717.0414-43

13. Airlift to Besieged Areas 7 April - 31 August 1972 (Declassified*), by Paul T. Ringenbach, 7 Dec 1973   K717.0414-33

14. Drug Abuse in Southeast Asia (Declassified), by Richard B. Carver, 1 Jan 1975   K717.0414-50

15. Aerial Protection of Mekong River Convoys in Cambodia (Declassified**), by Capt William A. Mitchell, 1 Oct 1971   K717.0414-23

*Declassification date incorrectly computed on cover of document.
**Declassified by Office of Air Force History, 2 May 1977

www.ingramcontent.com/pod-product-compliance
Lightning Source LLC
Chambersburg PA
CBHW080549170426
43195CB00016B/2729